Global Youth Work

Provoking Consciousness and Taking Action

Momodou Sallah

Russell House Publishing

First published in 2014 by:
Russell House Publishing Ltd.
58 Broad Street
Lyme Regis
Dorset DT7 3QF

Tel: 01297-443948
Fax: 01297-442722
e-mail: help@russellhouse.co.uk
www.russellhouse.co.uk

British Library Cataloguing-in-publication Data:
A catalogue record for this book is available from the British Library.

ISBN: 978-1-905541-87-4

Typeset by TW Typesetting, Plymouth, Devon

Printed by IQ Laserpress, Aldershot

About Russell House Publishing

Russell House Publishing aims to publish innovative and valuable materials to help managers, practitioners, trainers, educators and students.

Our full catalogue covers: families, children and young people; engagement and inclusion; drink, drugs and mental health; textbooks in youth work and social work; workforce development.

Full details can be found at www.russellhouse.co.uk and we are pleased to send out information to you by post. Our contact details are on this page.

We are always keen to receive feedback on publications and new ideas for future projects.

Contents

Introduction

The emerging discipline of Global Youth Work, as a distinct pedagogical approach to working with young people based on the principles of youth work and Development Education, has been shrouded in a lack of theoretical location, and largely relegated within the realms of practice. This book is my attempt to advance a conceptual framework for Global Youth Work, drawing on theories of globalisation, anti-oppressive practice, development, Education, and Youth Work. It is by no means a complete work, but one that builds on earlier efforts of others like Bourne and McCollum (1995).

Based on my experiences of teaching the Global Youth Work components of Youth and Community Work courses over the last nine years as well as having been in practice in this field for the last 20 years; and also being deeply involved in conducting groundbreaking research on Global Youth Work theory and practice and its efficacy as a pedagogical approach; this book reflects a collection of my thoughts and my encounters with this young emerging discipline. It should not be seen as an exhaustive project, but one that attempts to provide spaces and resources for youth workers, social workers, development workers, and associated trainees and academics within these fields, to critically engage with this discipline.

If nothing else, this book attempts to do two things, as indicated in the title, to provoke consciousness, and support people to take action.

First, this is premised on my encounters in research, teaching and practice, where the first objective of engagement is to get individuals and collective groups of young people to explore other possibilities of conceptualising and interacting with the world, different from their fixed constructions of reality, to gain a new critical consciousness. The case studies in this book are those that I have used in my teaching. Individual readers should also find them helpful.

The second objective is to move from what can at times be only defined as a state of paralysis, to change the way things are, commensurate with the young people's abilities.

Global Youth Work, I would argue, should also be rooted in social justice: social justice in a world of grotesque inequality and pervasive distribution of the world's resources; social justice for a world in which 80% of its resources are consumed by only 20% of its inhabitants; social justice for a scenario where 229 out of every 1000 children born in Mali in 1998–1999 would die before they reach their fifth birthday compared to 3 per 1000 live births in Sweden in 2002;

social justice for those who have continued to consume the toxic fumes of deprivation, hopelessness and helplessness; social justice for those who continue to bear witness to both within country and between country inequalities. Making social justice a central plank of our engagement in Global Youth Work means admitting that we can at times, given our *situatedness*, start from a position of *negative neutrality*; however, it means that we can provoke young people's consciousness to be able to conceive of alternative versions of reality, and navigate the complex matrix of global interconnectedness and the inextricability of their lives with that of others, from the food they eat, the clothes they wear, the energy they consume to the very political systems that facilitate their privilege or disadvantage, politically, economically, technologically, culturally and ecologically. In its attempt to develop a conceptual framework for Global Youth Work, this book introduces and explores a range of terms, ideas and ideologies.

In **Chapter 1**, the concept and process of globalisation is explored, highlighting the many definitions and configurations of globalisation. The chapter also presents the five faces of globalisation: how the process affects our existence economically, politically, environmentally, culturally and technologically. The many contested perspectives and interpretations of globalisation are presented, and the chapter concludes that the process of globalisation is inevitable and inescapable; however, practicing the domain of Global Youth Work requires us to be able to situate our praxis within a deep understanding of the concept and process of globalisation.

In **Chapter 2**, we explore the construction of social reality and how our spatial and experiential locations influence our reality. We explore the many professional and personal positions in relation to reality: relativism, dogmatism and cultural competence. This exploration is linked to the philosophical and ideological *situatedness* of the globaphiles, globaphobes and the globacritics. Ultimately, this chapter illustrates that reality is not a fixed and given entity; to the contrary, many practitioners position their stances of negative neutrality to be unquestionable. Global Youth Work questions this position and its hegemonic relationship with ideological situations of globalisation.

Chapter 3 explains inequality in totality: including definitions of inequality, both between and within country, as well as the scale and nature of global inequality. It explores the different dimensions of inequality, including health, education and access to quality of life. It goes on to establish the grotesque and disproportionate human and statistical face of inequality and lays bare the structures that engender global inequality. Ultimately this chapter positions development and social justice as antidotes to inequality, and premises Global

Youth Work on the need to redress inequality at the personal, local, national and global levels.

In **Chapter 4**, we explore the notion of development and sustainability, highlighting major developmental perspectives and the different dimensions of sustainability, including economic, political, social and environmental. We specifically address the ecological conundrum, and we position development and sustainability as contested and based on *situatedness*. This chapter questions development itself as well as what kind of development we intend to initiate as youth and community development practitioners.

Chapter 5 explores the sub-discipline of Global Youth Work and starts by providing definitions; it then explores the terminology of Global Youth Work versus underpinning conceptualisations. Major Global Youth Work conceptual models are reviewed and attempts to theorise Global Youth Work are made, culminating in the advancement of my five faces and PLiNGs model. Ultimately this chapter dissects the distinct practice of Global Youth Work as a methodology of working with young people to provoke consciousness and promote action, based on the principles of youth work and Development Education.

Chapter 6 presents the empiric evidence that establishes the efficacy of Global Youth Work as a pedagogical tool that effectively engages young people around local-global issues. In response to the dearth of empiric evidence in the wider field of youth work in general and Global Youth Work in particular, this chapter provides the needed evidence to back up claims of Global Youth Work's efficacy. It presents evidence from three separate research projects operationalised over the last five years with the intention to establish or otherwise debunk Global Youth Work's efficacy. After reviewing previous studies, the three research projects, with the biggest sample in the field so far, provide a view on the efficacy of Global Youth Work.

This book, whilst premised on the growing imperatives to address the global dimension of informal education with young people, has as a cardinal objective the need to develop both the theory and practice of Global Youth Work, to provoke consciousness and promote action based on the ownership of the process by those affected.

Momodou Sallah
January 2014

References

Bourne, D. and McCollum, A. (1995) *A World of Diference*. London: DEA.

About the Author

Dr Momodou Sallah is Senior Lecturer at the Youth and Community Division, De Montfort University. He has over twenty years' experience working with young people at the local, national and international levels. He has published extensively in the field of work with young people around globalisation and intercultural competence. His research interests include diversity, participation and globalisation in relation especially to young people. Dr Sallah is actively involved in advocacy and set up Global Hands, a Community Interest Company social enterprise, with former and current students at De Montfort University to challenge inequality both at the local and global levels. Momodou was awarded a National Teaching Fellowship in 2013.

Dedication

To the memories of uncle Omar Fofana and Omar Barrow.

Acknowledgements

Much gratitude for the invaluable contribution of Professor Simon Dyson to my professional growth; to the good people of Global Hands and my colleagues at DMU and the wider field. I would also like to express gratitude to the Y Care International project team and their support in carrying out the two DFID projects that form the basis of Chapter 6. I am grateful to Dr Viv Rolfe for all her support with the diagrams. To Kodou, Abdoulie, Sulayman and Cherno for their continued support.

Global Youth Work Drivers

This book is relevant to all those who work with young people globally.

The imperatives to address the global dimension of education in youth work have been set out in a number of key documents, for example those that are set out below. Although these particular documents are within the English context, this should not discourage readers from elsewhere.

The National Occupational Standards for Youth Work set the following objectives and outcomes:

- *Encourage young people to broaden their horizons to be active citizens*
- *Explore constructively with young people the concept of citizenship including its relevance at local, national and international levels*
- *Explore with young people the global context to personal, local and national decisions and actions.*

(LLUK, 2008)

The National Youth Agency (NYA) Professional Validation and Curriculum requirements call for the location of the 'international and global context' in programmes of study (NYA, 2007: 17).

The Youth Work Subject Benchmark urges practitioners to 'locate their practice within a matrix of power dynamics across the local, global and faith divides . . .' (QAA, 2009: 17). These imperatives are also covered in the Department for Education and Skills' *Common Core of Skills and Knowledge for the Children's Workforce* as well (DfES, 2005).

References

DfES (Department for Education and Skills) (2005) *Common Core of Skills and Knowledge for the Children's Workforce*. London: DFES.

LLUK (Lifelong Learning UK) (2008) *National Occupational Standards for Youth Work*. Available online from: www.lluk.org/national-occupational-standards.htm

NYA (National Youth Agency) (2007) *Introduction to Professional Validation and Curriculum Requirements (Book 1 of 3)*. Available online from http://www.nya.org.uk/information/108741/professionalvalidation/

QAA (Quality Assurance Agency for Higher Education) (2009) *Subject Benchmark Statement: Youth and Community Work*. Available online from http://www.qaa.ac.uk/academicinfrastructure/benchmark/honours/default.asp

CHAPTER 1

What is Globalisation?

Introduction

Globalisation affects every human being one way or the other, more so young people. Developing effective Global Youth Work praxis should be preceded by a critical understanding of both the concept and process of globalisation as well as how it impacts people at the personal, local, national and global levels. In this chapter we start by defining and then move on to the key characteristics of globalisation. From there, we explore globalisation as a concept and as a process, leading to the identification of the five faces of globalisation. The chapter concludes by arguing that globalisation as a process is inevitable and encourages students to build their own theory. What exactly is it? How did it start and how is it manifested in young people's everyday experiences?

Objectives

1. Understand the concept and process of globalisation.
2. Explore the five faces of globalisation.
3. Explore the different and opposing views in relation to globalisation.
4. Demonstrate the growing interdependency of the world.
5. Build our own theory of globalisation.

What is globalisation?

There are far too many definitions of globalisation to go through, which the scope of this book cannot cover. However, we will start by considering some practical examples in the following activity:

Activity 1.1

Consider the following questions and jot down your answers:
1. What is the relationship between the sub-prime mortgage crisis in America and the drop in house prices in England?
2. Where is your skirt/blouse/shirt made? What are the political, economic, cultural, environmental and technological considerations in relation to those who made these things and you wearing them?

---

3. With its roots in the Bronx, New York, how does hip-hop impact on the young
   people you work with?
After jotting down your answers, please try discussing them in small groups. Unpick
your answers by exploring and locating the active process of globalisation in your
everyday realities.

Comment

After Activity 1.1 you might notice and begin to draw out that there is a direct
correlation between the sub-prime mortgage crisis and house prices falling, the
economy faltering and people losing their jobs. This can also be directly
correlated to the value of the British Pound which affects the cost of goods
and the spending power of British tourists overseas. It has also led to houses
losing a significant portion of their values, and to first time buyers finding it
very difficult to buy a house as a result of a tighter credit regime.

In relation to your item of clothing, it is likely that you will notice that most
of your clothing is made from outside the UK, most notably China and Eastern
Europe. What you might also begin to observe are the trade implications –
technological, environmental, cultural and political (in terms of the negotiation
of trade rules and regulations) – of what you wear and those who make it.
Your item of clothing as an example can be replaced with fruits, cars or energy
to illustrate the point: that we depend on a number of countries to meet our
daily basic needs, and that there are different dimensions to transactions.

In relation to hip-hop with its origins in the Bronx, you might begin to draw out
that hip-hop is now a global phenomenon and technological advancements mean
that Fifty Cent's music can be heard instantly in all five continents; additionally
hip-hop is a lifestyle, including the political dimension of its lyrics as a protest against
the system, and its sense of clothing fuels a fashion industry with global implications.

From the three above scenarios, you might begin to locate how globalisation
works. The observation that the world is closer and people are more aware of
this, as well as being more interdependent, illustrates this point.

Globalisation therefore can be defined as a process by which the interaction
between people and nations is much closer; where time and distance are no
longer constraints; and which gravitates towards a global order. It means that
local and national boundaries no longer define the primary and exclusive
spaces of interaction; to the contrary, every local and national action and
reaction takes place in a more interactive and conscious global order. Let us for
a moment consider a number of definitions:

Activity 1.2

In small groups where possible, explore the following definitions and find their similarities and divergence. Where do they agree and where do they disagree?

A. 'In an economic context, (globalisation) is normally understood to mean a process of *increasing international interactions and acceleration of international trade, capital and information flows* but that globalization can also be seen to have a political dimension, including the *diffusion of global norms and values*, the spread of democracy and the proliferation of treaties' (House of Lords Select Committee on Economic Affairs, 2002: 12).

B. 'When you think about integration, it is something that has a number of dimensions and you can go a long way or a short way or a medium way on each dimension . . . the dimensions you can think about are trade which is one of the easiest to analyse and where the results are clearest, but *we also see globalisation of capital, some modest globalisation of labour and the globalisation of communications, technology, transport, crime and disease* and so on' (Nicholas Stern, World Bank Chief Economist and Senior Vice President in House of Lords Select Committee on Economic Affairs, 2002: 12).

C. 'Globalisation as a concept refers *both to the compression of the world and the intensification of consciousness of the world as a whole . . . increasing acceleration in both concrete global interdependence and consciousness of the global whole*' (Robertson, 1990: 8).

D. 'It is widely asserted that we live in an era in which *the greater part of social life is determined by global processes, in which national cultures, national economies and national borders are dissolving*' (Hirst and Thompson, 2002: 1).

E. '*A social process in which the constraints of geography on economy, political, social and cultural arrangements recede*, in which people become increasingly aware that they are receding and in which people act accordingly' (Waters, 2002: 5).

F. 'The intensification of worldwide social relations which link distant localities in such a way that local happenings are shaped by events occurring many miles away and vice versa' (Giddens, 1990: 64).

After discussing them in your groups, or reflecting on them individually, you may like to list on a flipchart the commonalities in the definitions as well as the differences.

Comment

While your group discussions or individual reflections would have been guided by your experiences and understanding of globalisation so far, some points of convergence and divergence might however begin to emerge which might include the following themes:

Integration

The world is getting closer by the day, and we are all being inserted into one indivisible world order; more importantly consciousness of that fact is correspondingly increasing. As Beck argues, globalisation:

> . . . *replaces the image of separate individual societies with one of a world-system in which everything – every society, every government, every company, every culture, every class, every household, every individual – must insert and assert itself within a single division of labour.*

(Beck, 2000: 32)

This integration of the world has many dimensions and is not solely limited to the economy and finance, it incorporates culture, politics, music, technology and travel. A criticism often levelled at this idea is that the integration of the world often serves only the interests of the rich and powerful, as a significant percentage of humanity is still cut off from the basics of telephone, flying and the Internet.

Interconnectedness

We as individuals, local communities, nation states and continents are inextricably linked together and the survival of one grossly affects that of everyone else. For example, poor market practices in the US fatally infected and affected market prices in the UK (house prices went down by 13.3 per cent, in the year up to September 2008) as well as leading to shares plunging across the globe (Hopkins and Ramnarayan, 2008). This, for example, not only affected the global economy, but also led to the sharp increase in unemployment nationally, and the closure of companies locally as well; this further led to mothers and fathers of young people being made redundant and/or losing their houses as a result. We are all so interconnected that one action in one part of the world greatly affects others at the other end of the earth.

When the H1N1 influenza virus, commonly known as swine flu, broke out in Veracruz, Mexico in April 2009, it affected all five continents of the earth deeply. Not only was it necessary for public health officials in Mexico to take drastic action, it also led to most countries and international bodies like the World Health Organisation and the European Union putting measures in place to protect their populations. In a literal sense, when Veracruz sneezed, the rest of the world caught a cold. This also led to massive abandonment of pre-booked holidays to Mexico by significant numbers of tourists from different parts of the world. It also led to a great mobilisation of the public, especially in schools and work places as well as youth and community centres, to combat the threat of the swine flu; in some instances schools were closed for days when an outbreak of swine flu was established. This illustrates, as earlier argued, that the world is now so interconnected, because of the accelerated pace and intensification of interaction, that we basically live quite literally in one world. Mathew Taylor's definition of globalisation perhaps captures this best: *'we all play in each others' backyards and the fences have been torn down between the gardens'* (Mathew Taylor MP, House of Lords Select Committee on Economic Affairs, 2002: 12).

Conquered distance, space, and time

Distance, space, and time are no longer barriers in worldwide interaction as technological advancements have made it much easier for people at two extreme ends of the earth to communicate instantaneously. Giddens (2002) explains that one could understand this instantaneous surge given that the first satellite was launched in 1969 and now there are over 200 such satellites above the earth; additionally, 'no dedicated transatlantic or transpacific cables existed at all until the late 1950s. The first held fewer than 100 voice paths. Those of today carry more than a million' (Giddens, 2002: 11).

This not only helps the economic/business interests to expand but extends to social, cultural and political exchanges as well. Globalisation has closely been linked to the 'death of distance' which means that time and distance have both been conquered and it is therefore no longer an obstacle in human interaction. This further means that the divide between people 'out there' and us 'in here' is less palpable since that barrier has been overcome by instantaneous communication through technological advancements.

Borderless state

When we talk about a 'borderless state', it often means that national boundaries or geographical spaces no longer limit the movement of people, goods, services, relationships and interactions, as these have become transnationally seamless. It also means that the background against which we think and act has increasingly moved from just the national to the global. However it can be argued that whilst the movement of people, goods and services from the West to the developing countries is often unhindered, this can at times be a one way street with the traffic from the opposite direction often limited by border controls and trade restrictions. Whilst technological advancements, especially the Internet, compel us to act and react in the domain of a borderless state, some people, especially from the West, have greater access to this *borderlessness* than others. In running Transnational Corporations (TNCs) now, it is no longer necessary to fly thousands of miles, spend thousands of dollars and in many instances days, to attend meetings; it is now possible to hold video conferences with people from all five continents participating simultaneously. Distance, space and time are no longer barriers in these instances.

A global agenda

This point argues that we can no longer be isolated into our localities and national realities alone, untouched by the hands of globalisation. Agendas have become globalised, like the global 'War on Terror'. Whether one agrees with the principles and methodologies used to pursue it or not, as well as its legality or illegality, it affects how we view the world and it affects others' reactions to the citizens of the West. Global diseases like Aids and the example given earlier in relation to swine flu illustrate the construction of a global agenda in need of a global response. In a similar vein, there is a global need to deal with the sub-prime mortgage crisis emanating from the US and its attendant consequences, as most countries are affected to various degrees.

The issue of high carbon emissions and the depletion of the ocean layer, leading to flooding, exposure to ultra violet rays and the extinction of endangered spices as a result of the destruction of their habitats has lead to a global agenda on climate change. The Kyoto Protocol to prevent climate change and global warming ran out in 2012 and in anticipation of its end, a climate change conference took place from the 6–18 of December, 2009 hosted by the Danish government in Copenhagen. 8,000 people took part, representing 170 countries, nongovernmental organisations and other elements of civil society. This is an example of the growing need to deal with issues at the global level with a global agenda. It will be futile to some extent for the West to deal with the issue of high carbon emissions alone, without the involvement of the rest of the world, especially the Asian giants of China and India; the reverse can also be said. Therefore, meaningful attempts to address what might traditionally have been construed as local and regional problems have now been recognised as global, because they are of concern to all of humanity, requiring a global response, hence the global agenda.

Power from the people, power to the TNC

What's the difference between Tanzania and Goldman Sachs? One is an African country that makes $2.2 billion a year and shares it among 25 million people. The other is an investment bank that makes $2.6 billion and shares most of it between 161 people.

(George in Pilger, 2001)

It has been argued that globalisation has led to Transnational Corporations (TNC) being able to operate businesses across many nations, and therefore wielding considerable budgets and correspondingly considerable power to make decisions. A number of TNCs have bigger budgets than some nation states (for example Nigeria is ranked 58th richest, with $41.1 billion, compared to Wal-Mart Stores at 44 with $67.7 billion; General Motors is ranked 53rd with $46.2 billion, compared with Ukraine ranked 66th with $35.3 billion). As they are also able to decide where jobs go and where investments are made, it is often asserted that some TNCs have now become more powerful than some nation states (Wolf, 2002 in Held and McGrew, 2007: 105). However, Held and McGrew (2007) argue that corporations do not rule the world, as the 40 top ranked are all nation states. The difference is that most governments to some extent have been mandated by the people in a mostly democratic process, whilst TNCs on the other hand are only accountable to their shareholders, guided by the principle of profit.

Capitalist hegemony

Building on from the last point, the dominant world order since the collapse of Communism in the mid-80s has been Capitalism which is premised on the dictates of a free market and the 'Washington Consensus' (Scholte, 2005). Crudely translated, this is tantamount to leaving everything at the hands of the market. The major criticism of this is that Capitalism has neither a heart nor a soul: it is primarily guided by the dictum of profit at all cost and consequently to the detriment of those oppressed and less well off. It is further argued that this further aggravates the gaps of within country and between country inequalities. This capitalist hegemony has been the target of virulent anti-capitalist protests during most May Day and G8 meetings, such as: the protests against the annual IMF and World Bank meetings that took place in Berlin in

1988; the powerful demonstrations against the 50th anniversary of the IMF and World Bank in Madrid in 1994; the Genoa 2001 protests against the G8; and perhaps the best known of all, the Seattle demonstrations against the WTO meeting which started on 30th November 1999, and which perhaps received more coverage than any previous demonstration in the media. One of the latest demonstrations took place in June 2013 when protesters attempted to occupy about a hundred buildings in the West End of London in an effort to attack symbols of capitalism. All of these demonstrations evidence the physical manifestations of anger often directed against the globalisation of capital and the capitalist stranglehold on it, to facilitate capitalism for the poor and socialism for the rich (such as state bail-outs of the banks) (Pilger, 2001). However some have argued that the introduction of Corporate Social Responsibility (CSR) has countered this and has given capitalism a more humane face (Patten, 2008). An example of CRS in practice is that of Salesforce.com, a global on-demand software Service Company which applies a formula of 1/1/1. This means that 1 per cent of its profits in the form of products, 1 per cent of its employee's time and 1 per cent of its equity goes to charities and nongovernmental organisations. Whilst this initiative is exceptional, it is often not the experience of many who criticise capitalist hegemony, and some critics question the real purpose of such magnanimity.

Process and concept of globalisation

It is important here to try to distinguish between the concept and process of globalisation. The concept refers to the coinage and articulation of *globalisation* as an idea, whilst the process is of it actually happening. The roots of the word globalisation can be traced back to McLuhan (1964) and Moore (1966). Waters (2001) suggested that the term was first used by The Economist (4/4/59) to report Italy's 'globalised quota' and Webster's was the first major dictionary to offer definitions of globalisation in 1961. In relation to its being a process, it is stated that:

> *Two dates – 1494 and 1969 – stand out as important moments in the history of the world as a global place . . . Since the Fifteenth Century, people have slowly come to think of the world as a global place. This process was aided by the widespread use of maps and globes in schoolrooms . . . [in 1969] the astronaut's photographs of the earth gave currency to the idea of the world as a global place.*
>
> (Schaffer, 1996: 10–11 in Habibul et al., 2000: 17)

Old wine in a new bottle?

Do you remember the Nina, Pinta and Santa Maria? These were the three ships that Christopher Columbus set sail with to circumnavigate the earth in the Fifteenth Century, and some would argue that that era of Spanish and Portuguese exploration to discover trade routes was the start of the process of globalisation hence the 'globe'; other notable explorers of the era included Vasco da Gama and Alvise Cadamosto, whilst other people (Frank and Gills, 1996; Tehranian, 1998) argue that the process is over 5000 years old. Yet more commentators link the start of the process to the industrial revolution which heralded a new dawn in a mechanised agrarian era epitomised by the building of faster machines including the steamship and the railway.

Yet others advance a view that the process of globalisation began between 1870–1914, the period often described as the 'Era of classical gold standard' when there were no major wars taking place and trade was at its most prosperous, unhindered by protectionism. The first catalyst for this phase was:

> *The development of transportation and communication networks that physically linked together different parts of the planet, especially by railways, shipping and the telegraph. The second was rapid growth of trade with its accompanying pattern of dependency, especially between the relatively industrialized countries of Western Europe and the rest. The third was a huge flow of capital mainly in the form of direct investment by European firms in non-industrialised areas.*
>
> (Barraclough, 1978 in Waters, 2001: 27)

It has been said that there was a 'Retreat into Nationalism' and 'rising protectionism' between 1914 and 1945 which ended the first wave of globalisation. This was because of the two world wars and the depression in between the wars. However, the second wave of globalisation, between 1945 and 1980, was a period of prosperity and led to rapid technological advancements, and some people argue that this is the real start of globalisation (Waters, 2001; Robertson, 1992). This could be attributed to the fact that the US emerged from the Second World War with the most powerful economy and was largely able to dictate terms of trade, especially with the establishment of the General Agreement on Tariffs and Trade (GATT) in 1947 now called the World Trade Organisation (WTO), leading to trade liberalisation, given the demise of the influential Soviet empire in the 1980s. Some commentators might suggest that the Soviet Union was in a similar position as the US in terms of being able to shape the forces of globalisation but Giddens (2002) offers an explanation as to why it was not:

The former Soviet Union and the East European countries were comparable to the West in terms of growth rates until somewhere around the early 1970s. After that point, they fell rapidly behind. Soviet communism, with its emphasis on state run enterprise and heavy industry could not compete in the global electronic economy. The ideological and cultural control upon which community political authority was based similarly could not survive in an era of global media.

(Giddens, 2002: 14)

Whilst it can be argued that all of the previous stages can, to some degree, be classified as starting the process, it was the post-1980 period when developing countries broke into the global markets, especially the Asian Tigers, as well as the collapse of the Soviet Republic in the mid-1980s, that really established globalisation as a process. This was speeded up with the advent of the Internet and other technological advancements in the 1990s.

In exploring the concept and process of globalisation, it can be stated that although the process is at least over 400 years old and some might say 5000 years, its use gained currency in the mid 1980s (Roberston, 1992; Waters, 2001). Whatever era gave birth to globalisation as a concept or process, what most commentators have been able to agree on is that it is now a reality and is here to stay. However it is also important to recognise that there is a school of thought that speaks of a post-globalisation era; basically that globalisation was over post 9/11 (Ferguson, 2005).

The majority of people I come across in teaching globalisation/Global Youth Work mostly associate globalisation with economics and finance; mostly limited to the impact of Transnational Corporations (e.g. Nike, GAP, Nestle) or how the Bretton Woods Institutions (IMF, World Bank, WTO) 'exploit' or 'support'

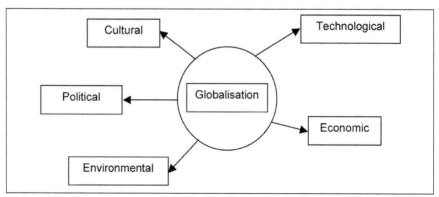

Figure 1.1   The five faces of globalisation

developing countries, depending on whether one tows the globaphile or globaphobic line. However, as you might have noticed by now, one could argue that in addition to the economic face, there are also the environmental, political, cultural and technological faces. **The economic face** is a cardinal component of globalisation, as it can be argued it is the most visible and is often the focus of protest against Capitalism. The movement of 'mobile stateless capital' since the 1970s also makes multinational/transnational branding and invasion of traditionally national domains more visible, like Coca Cola invading the Indian market to the detriment of local industries. The economic face, as earlier argued, is the financial dimension to do with trade in goods and services across nations; it can be about the local impacting on the global, as well as the global impacting on the local (Beynon and Dunkerley, 2000).

The **environmental face** of globalisation is also visible as people increasingly grapple with the destruction of their environment. This destruction is strongly linked to carbon emission, destruction of the ozone layer as well as destruction of the rain forest resulting in global warming, exposure to harmful ultraviolet rays, flooding and even to the quality of air we breathe. This environmental face is the focus of many environmental campaigners like Greenpeace.

The **cultural face** of globalisation is also not something that is new; it might have gone by the name of 'cultural imperialism' in the past. This face is about how culture, which can broadly be defined as a people's way of life, is diffused through technological advancement and is often propagated from a particular perspective as the pinnacle. This can be in the area of food, for example: how MacDonald's might be promoted as the 'cool' and 'ideal' thing to have; in the shape of beauty, where size zero models are pushed as the ideal of beauty; or even in the diffusion of a gangster culture through the music of Fifty Cent (the 'get rich or die trying' attitude) through lyrics, dressing and life outlook. This dimension of globalisation uses existing media, like the Internet, satellite TV and other instantaneous means of communication, to promote a cultural dogma, mainly from the North to the detriment of the South.

The **technological face** is the main vehicle transmitting the cultural dogma; it embodies all means of communication bringing the world together and especially bringing people from distant lands to be in touch instantly. This includes the Internet, satellite, mobile phones, teleconferencing, newspapers and fashion magazines and air travel in all its manifestations.

Giddens (2002: 10) puts forward a scenario which illustrates this point very well. He gave the example of a trillion (a million million) dollars being turned

Global Youth Work

over every day in global currency markets. Having this amount of money physically in one place would mean having a pile of cash '120 miles high, 20 times higher than Mount Everest'. Given the magnitude of this, which is a huge increase from as recently as 1980, it is interesting to note that electronic money, 'money that only exist as digits in computers' makes the present nature of the 'new global electronic economy' possible (Giddens, 2002: 9).

Last but by no means least is the **political face**. This includes the diffusion of certain 'democratic' values and the management of geo-politics. It captures the postulation of what is right and wrong and how world order is dictated; it defines what human rights abuse is and what brand of 'democracy' is acceptable and exportable. It also greatly incorporates the functions, successes and frustrations of the UN.

It should be noted that these different faces do not stand alone; they are mostly interlinked and symbiotic. For example, you cannot separate the technological from the cultural in the globalisation of hip-hop, or separate the political from the cultural in the mass exportation of 'democratic norms and values'. To deal with Global Youth Work requires an understanding of the five faces of globalisation and how they affect young people at the personal, local, national and global levels; otherwise it becomes very difficult to break down big abstract concepts at the global level and make them relevant to the young people we work with at the individual and group levels.

The debate: globaphiles vs. globaphobes

You would have seen from the definitions in Activity 1.2 that there are often heated and vitriolic arguments as to whether globalisation is a good or bad thing. Globaphiles, often known as proponents, believe that the process of globalisation is very good for human civilisation and development and therefore must be supported. On the other hand, globaphobes, often labelled sceptics, believe that it is one of the worse afflictions ever to be cast on the human race.

Activity 1.3

This exercise can be done individually or in a group. When done in a group, the whole group should stand in a straight line and decide where each is on the global continuum. After considering the two sides of the debate, where do you stand?

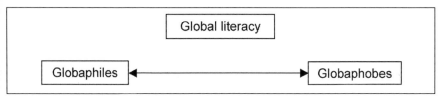

Figure 1.2 Global literacy continuum

Activity 1.3 involves making an individual decision and must be informed by one's individual experiences and understanding. Some people will move their positions at different stages of their study and practice and this is OK; the dangerous thing is to remain stationary even when there is compelling evidence to move you. A fundamental component of youth work is the ability to reflect on action and the deconstruction of one's reality resulting in a change of values and attitudes. The most important element at this stage is understanding what informs each person's world view and consequently informs their values and attitudes, as the focus should be on each individual. The facilitator should get everyone to reflect on why they are standing where they are standing, and to share the reason with the group. Whilst globaphobia and globaphilia are the two extremes, it is very important to note these are not the only stances; to the contrary, a middle stance can be adopted where the potential for globalisation to be both good and bad can be acknowledged as a result of a critical understanding of the concept and process; this I call *global literacy*. Global competency incorporates the ability to take action – having the required skills, knowledge and resources. This will be covered in greater detail in the next chapters.

The inevitability of globalisation

I will conclude by stating that globalisation has brought our interactions and reactions closer, and whilst some benefit from it, there are clearly those who are disadvantaged by it. It can be argued that there is no escaping the process of globalisation, even if one withdraws from humanity and indulges in a caveman/woman-like existence; the economic, political, cultural, environmental and technological impact of the process of globalisation will be visited on us.

In this light, the significance of understanding the impact of globalisation on the lives of the young people we work with cannot be overemphasised; both the concept and process must be understood in order to effectively locate its impact on the lives of young people. This will lead to effective Global Youth Work.

Activity 1.4

What is your theory of globalisation
- In groups of five and using any preferred medium (drama, poster, poetry, rap etc.), present your theory of globalisation to the class (using the learning from the chapter and your general knowledge).
- You should first of all get into your group and articulate your views before propagating your theory.
- You have five minutes to present to the rest of the class.

After each presentation, the facilitator and the rest of the class should ask for clarification, and should challenge the theory advanced. The aim of this exercise is to explore learning so far and how we start to develop our own theory of globalisation. This is pivotal as a basis for the effective delivery of Global Youth Work.

References

Beck, U. (2000) *What is Globalization?* Cambridge: Polity Press.
Beynon, J. and Dunkerley, D. (Eds.) (2000). *Globalization: The Reader*. New York: Routledge.
Ferguson, N. (2005) Sinking Globalisation. *Foreign Affairs*, 84: 2, 64–77.
Frank, A.G. and Gills, B.K. (1996) *The World System: Five Hundred Years or Five Thousand?* London: Routledge.
Giddens, A. (1990) *The Consequences of Modernity*. Stanford: Stanford University Press.
Giddens, A. (2002) *Runaway World: How Globalisation is Shaping Our Lives*. London: Profile Books.
Habibul, H.K. (2000) Globalization: Against Reductionism and Linearity. *Development and Society*, 29: 1, 17–33.
Held, D. and McGrew, A. (2007) *Globalization/Anti-globalisation: Beyond the Great Divide*. Cambridge: Polity.
Hirst, P. and Thompson, G. (2002) The Future of Globalization. *Cooperation and Conflict*, 37: 3, 252–3.
Hopkins, K. and Ramnarayan, A. (2008) *The Guardian* www.guardian.co.uk/money/2008/oct/15/property-housing-market. Accessed 26/10/08
House of Lords Select Committee on Economic Affairs (2002) *Globalisation*. London: HMSO.
McLuhan, M. (1964) *Understanding Media*. London: Routledge and Kegan Paul.
Moore, W. (1966) Global Sociology: The World as a Singular System. *American Journal of Sociolnogy*, 71, 5: 475–82.
Patten, C. (2008) *What Next? Surviving the Twenty-first Century*. Allen Lane/Blackwell.
Pilger, J. (2001) *New Rulers of the World*. ITV video.
Robertson, R. (1992) *Globalization: Social Theory and Global Culture*. London: Sage.
Scholte, J. A. (2005) *Globalisation: A Critical Introduction*. Basingstoke: Palgrave
Tehranian, M. (1998) Globalism, Localism and Islamism: Migration, Identity and World System Development. *International Political Science Review*, March.
Waters, M. (2001) *Globalization*. New York: Routledge.

CHAPTER 2

Construction of Social Reality

Introduction

Our understanding of the concept and process of globalisation is a prerequisite to carrying out effective Global Youth Work. A key plank of this critical understanding of globalisation requires us to locate the different ways in which this process is experienced across cultures, countries and realities. In this light, this chapter will seek to explore the construction of social reality and its variations dependent on spatial and experiential location. It will then argue that reality and the dismantling of that reality, what some might call education, is not a neutral process, but one imbued with and determined by our experiences of globalisation. We will then explore a range of case studies to illustrate the very process of constructing and deconstructing reality. In conclusion, we will finally explore the extreme stances of relativism and dogmatism in the construction of social reality and the need to cultivate global literacy and competence.

Objectives

1. To engage the learner in critically exploring the construction of social reality and how this impacts on various people's experiences of globalisation.
2. To support the learner in building a critical understanding of various reactions to globalisation, on the basis of which their practice can be built.
3. To demonstrate that the 'reality' that we take for granted is not a given, but constructed through 'human meaning making'.

What is social reality?

I would contend that whatever view we hold of globalisation, whether we believe it to be a force for good or evil, is largely based on our view of the world or what I would like to call our construction of social reality. In order for us to understand the contrasting positions of the globaphobes and the globaphiles, as well as develop effective Global Youth Work practice, it is cardinal that we understand how the holders of these extreme positions construct their realities.

Youth workers, as Davies (2005) argues, ply their trade of supporting young people's personal and social development by starting from their territory, literally and metaphorically, and 'tipping the balance of power' in the young person's favour. This process requires the youth worker to understand young people's realities as well as his/her own reality in relation to the world. Without an accurate location of reality, intervention in the lives of young people becomes misplaced.

It is pivotal to state from the onset that people's understanding and interpretation of globalisation, and therefore their reaction to it, is often determined by their experiences; and invariably by their construction of social reality and the 'human meaning making' (Rogers, 1989: 26) attached to this experience. Reality, how you see the world and the value positions you take, what is right or wrong, good or bad, just or unjust, is not constructed in a vacuum. These views are based upon layers and layers of experiences, built up over many years, and these then coalesce to form a 'reality', which becomes the basis on which you 'see' and interact with the world. In a similar vein, people's experiences of globalisation will most likely determine their perspective of globalisation, whether it is good or bad. For example, for someone who lives in the West and has largely experienced the fruits of globalisation, such as cheap holidays to exotic destinations, enjoying the best foods from all over the world at below production prices, and whose transportation has been made available by the technological dimension of globalisation, their experience of globalisation would most likely be great and positive. On the other hand, for someone who has borne witness to the brutal capitalist machinery in operation, for example where someone from the South has seen how the economic dimension of globalisation and the neoliberal project has destroyed their forest in the exploitation of timber for the West, or overgrazing by cattle to feed the MacDonald's restaurants' quest for beef burgers, then their experience will obviously be different. These examples do not mean that everyone from the West benefits from globalisation and everyone from the South does not; to the contrary, whilst people's experiences and construction of reality can sometimes be collective, it is often personal. Additionally, inequality affects citizens of a country in different ways. Between-country inequality exists between two different countries, for example the inequality that exists between UK and Senegal. On the other hand, within-country inequality focuses on the inequality that exists between the different citizens of a country; for example, 'the poorest 5 per cent of Frenchmen have a mean income which places them at the 72nd percentile of world income distribution;

the richest 5 percent have an income which places them in the top percentile of the world' (Milanovic, 2006: 143). This point illustrates the fact that living in a Western or affluent country does not necessarily guarantee benefiting from the country's wealth or the process of globalisation, even though this is a more likely scenario for someone who lives in the West. This same logic can be applied to the different ways in which people have experienced and continue to experience the process of globalisation. We can thus begin to speak of situatedness in relation to people's experiences and realities when considering the impact of globalisation.

Case studies

Activity 2.1

In your groups, please have a look at one or all of the attached case studies and try answering the following:

1. How do you feel about these views? What are your raw reactions to them?
2. Do you agree with the views expressed?
3. Is that reality different from yours?
4. Are these views right or wrong?

Draw a poster to answer the above questions as well as demonstrate your understanding of how social reality is constructed.

Case 1

It's gone past midnight but I still cannot sleep; I am so full of excitement that I might explode any minute. Tomorrow is the big day when I shall be circumcised; when I shall cross the border between girlhood and womanhood and assume my rightful place in the community. My name is Aminata and I am twelve years old. I live in a small village in Southern Senegal called Sare Pateh. If you are not circumcised then you will be considered unclean and no man would want to marry you; no one dares think of not getting circumcised because you will bring shame on your family.

Case 2

My brother's just taken his fourth wife and the celebration is ongoing; this is the seventh day and the dancing, drumming, eating and singing! Wow, what a big man my brother is! Although I am only ten, I want to be just like him when I grow up, and marry four wives. My religion permits it and you get more respect in the community; additionally you get to have loads of children who can help out in the farm. Oh God, how I admire him.

Case 3

I am sick and tired of these f**king immigrants, why the f**k can't they go home with their smelly food and stinking houses. Why can't they go home? All they do is sponge off the system, stay on benefits and breed like mice to occupy all available council houses. You know what, we should send all of them home; throw their f**king arses back to the trees they come from. All this political correctness is getting to my head!

Case 4

They say I am angry! They accuse me of organising the masses and stirring trouble but how can I not? Officials of the present government are stooges who are being used to subjugate their own people like all the other peoples of the world. They came, you know who I mean, Western governments! Ever since they came, they have been raping and pillaging our land and exploiting our people; destroying our way of life in the name of development. They use institutions like the IMF and the World Bank to introduce Structural Adjustment Programmes (SAP), Economic Recovery Programmes (ERP) and Programmes for Sustained Development (PSD) to starve my people! You know what these programmes mean? Removal of local subsidies, currency devaluation and unfair trading orchestrated by the World Trade Organisation. The British and the Americans, they are all the same, bloodsuckers!

Case 5

The only way to strike at the heart of the infidels is to blow myself up and take as many of them as possible. The havoc they have wreaked against the *Ummah* – Palestine, Afghanistan and Iraq – is unacceptable! Death to them all. A few more steps, and oblivion. God is Great!

Case 6

Although I don't love him, I have to marry him for the interest of my family; my parents have already given their word and it will definitely advance my family status. I cannot imagine sleeping with and waking up next to a man I do not love, every day for the rest of my life, but I will do it for my family. What I want as an individual is secondary to our best interest as a family.

In doing the above exercise, it is important that we are totally honest with ourselves, and where this exercise is being done in a group or in class, that a safe academic learning zone is created where our political correctness is left at the door and we come in naked to expose our true selves. This process can only be positive as it would lead to two outcomes: one is that our way of seeing the world is validated after some rigorous tests, or our way of seeing the world is flawed when exposed to a critical interrogation. This can sometimes be a painful and uncomfortable process as what we have come to accept as normal, and constructed to be right or wrong, is turned on its head.

Commentary on the case studies

How do you feel about these views? What are your raw reactions to them?

In reflecting on the above, some readers might find female circumcision or the extreme of female genital mutilation abhorrent or revolting; in fact it might be beyond some readers' ability to even conceptualise such a possibility. These case studies have been explored with students over many years and initial raw reactions in the case of the above, as well as in that of the suicide bomber, are often of 'revulsion', 'disgust', that it is 'barbaric' and 'uncivilised'. Again, these reactions might be the reality of those removed from the world of those in the case studies, perhaps of someone located somewhere in Middle England, or those of someone living in an outer estate in the UK, and whose livelihood is threaten by the 'influx of immigrants'. These raw feelings contrast the different ways in which social reality is constructed and, on the same basis, how the world is interacted with, from different realities.

Do you agree with the views expressed?

Again putting all notions of political correctness aside, readers are encouraged to state clearly whether they can relate to the realities in the case studies. I have explored these case studies over six years with people from many walks of life including students, practitioners, policy makers and academics in many different countries and from many backgrounds. However the initial reaction I mostly encounter is that of many people hesitating to answer the question straightforwardly, with an attempt to justify and qualify their answers. Whilst this is definitely considerate, it points to a tendency in some cases to be relative and sing the political correctness song.

Is that reality different from yours?

In some cases, these case studies might be your reality; but in most cases, especially for the majority of people living in the UK, they probably will not be. However, it is important to understand that a significant number of people in the UK are affected by some of these issues, like forced marriage, a disdain of immigrants, female circumcision, polygamy, Multinational Corporations and Transnational Corporations' exploitation. These examples might not necessarily affect the dominant population, but they are definitely significant. Additionally, engaging with Global Youth Work requires us to deconstruct our own reality, as well as deconstructing the reality of others as a starting point.

Are these views right or wrong?

This is a question that is difficult to answer as the question is in itself relative; if we were to take a philosophical approach then perhaps it will take eternity to find an answer. In relation to the six case studies, people might take different positions.

As highlighted in the Cultural competence continuum diagram opposite (Figure 2.1), one of these positions might be relativism, in that some readers' reaction might be that it is other people's culture and they know best. Whilst this approach can be non-judgemental, it can potentially be described as professional inertia, where the practitioner lets everything go by without critical interrogation because it is the point of least resistance.

At the other extreme end of the continuum, we can come across views that can be described as being dogmatic; in that the dominant reality, which in this case might be a Eurocentric one, becomes the only prism through which the world is seen. Everything not aligned to this constructed reality then becomes wrong. Whilst people who take this approach might be quite clear, with a definite sense of right or wrong and be decisive in their approach, their dogmatic approach caters for very little by way of the complex and multiple ways in which reality is constructed.

The third way I would advocate is that of cultural competence and global literacy, where the balance is struck between having a clear sense of right and wrong as well as being open to multiple realities. It is one that calls for a recalibration of approaches to perceived differences and diversity and one that allows the practitioner to gain the required skills, knowledge, values and resources to effectively operate across localities, nationalities and realities.

From the above exercise, it is thus easy to understand the fixed and immobile ways in which reality can be constructed. This can be from the missionary position (Sallah, 2008b) where development interventions are premised on a colonial and missionary position of Christianising and civilising 'these poor souls'; implicit in this approach is the premise that our way of seeing the world is the right way and others' is the wrong way. Javier Solana (2010) argues for a process of de-Westernisation to counter what can be labelled as a dogmatic

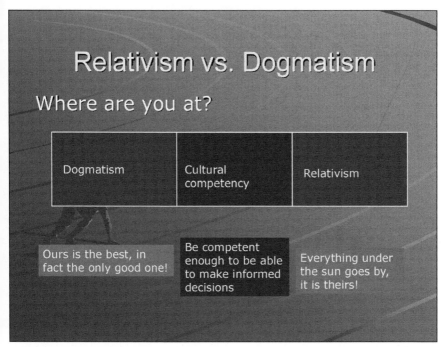

Figure 2.1 Cultural competence continuum

view, which considers that constructing reality through the Western prism as being the final frontier of truth. Oakley (1981) espouses the concept of Cultural Affinity, and Boushel (2000) talks about Experiential Affinity: in both cases, these are ways in which the person constructs the people they are researching. By extension, having an affinity or deep understanding of reality from the point of view of those in whose lives we intervene, is a *sine qua non*, especially in the context of cross-cultural global interventions.

Ideology and normalisation

Thompson (2003) construes oppression and discrimination as being operated at the personal, cultural and structural levels. The cultural and structural levels denote a constructed normality, a permeating social reality. Althusser's (1971) work presents his thesis of the Repressive State Apparatus and the Ideological State Apparatuses. The former, he argues, functions through violence, like the police, the administration and the army. The latter, his thesis holds, is soft-core and functions through ideology and is effected through media and religious outlets, for example. His premise is that reality and its enaction can be enforced: both through the violence of the state, even if this 'violence' of the state takes non-physical forms such as the role of the administration; and through the ideological apparatuses which are less visible and implicitly more difficult to pinpoint. These ideological state apparatuses can be manifested in a number of ways, ranging from personal beliefs to ideologies embedded within the state, and are increasingly significant, global structures. Within a quite different research tradition, Berger and Luckmann (1967) write on the construction of social reality, suggesting that the development of human meaning-making is based on our experiences, how the world is socially constructed and how we interact with it. Within these conceptual constructs, there is an implicit and explicit construction of normality, difference and the 'other' (Said, 1998). Everything that resides within the cultural and structural is conceived of as normal, and everything outside the boundary is conceived of as abnormal and different – a process of 'othering' (Sallah, 2009b). This paradigm might be construed as dichotomous between one extreme of a continuum and another. However, the paradigm of 'othering' is more adequately conceptualised as one that is contingent and fluid, and dependent on the numerous variables at play: race, class, gender, nationality, ideology, sexuality and sexual orientation amongst others. I would therefore argue that reality, or normality as labelled above in this paragraph, does not only operate at the individual level but can be embedded in a people's collective self and for that matter can be internalised as self evident.

Negative neutrality

In this light, and given my experience in practice, research and teaching, my analysis leads me to the conclusion of a thesis I want to advance as Negative Neutrality. Freire (1972) argues, incisively, that education is political and cannot be neutral. In my practice and interaction with academia, I have come across the dominant view that education, and by extension, intervention in young people's lives, should be objective and neutral. However, when one reflects on the starting point of what one considers to be neutral, then it is possible to deduct that that starting point of neutrality is not itself totally neutral as it is imbued by our experiences of constructed reality and our sense of situatedness. I shall illustrate this point with the diagram below. In Figure 2.2, we see that zero is the perfect starting point and going to the left accumulates negative numbers and going to the right denotes positive numbers. So it is easy to assume that the views we hold and the intervention that accompanies it starts

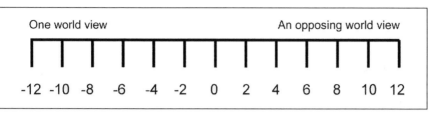

Figure 2.2 Negative neutrality

from a complete point of neutrality, when in actual fact it might be starting from, say, +2 or −3.

Consequently we can speak of negative neutrality where the practitioner assumes that their engagement with young people to address global issues starts from a position of 0 on the number line. However, this reality is often constructed from a perspective which sees and interacts with the world in a particular way that is not neutral. It is a negative neutrality.

Intercultural competence and global literacy

It is important that we understand when dealing with people from different backgrounds and countries, as we are bound to do in an increasingly globalised world, especially in the field of Global Youth Work, that reality is not fixed and that our 'reality' is located within our experiences; we should exercise, in this impasse of the realities presented by the young people, what Cunha and Gomes (2010: 86) call 'tolerance of ambiguity'. Tolerance of ambiguity has been explained by Otten (2010) as the ability to:

> On the one hand, recognise cultural differences amongst European societies and communities; (and) on the other hand, acknowledge the intrinsic uncompleted character of each cultural system and, therefore, acceptance of the ambiguity and multiple uncertainties generated by the cultural encounters.

As such, 'tolerance of ambiguity', 'solidarity' and 'empathy' could be understood as aspects of intercultural competence (in Hoskins and Sallah, 2011: 118). It is essential for the reader to understand that in working across cultures, countries and realities, taking 'reality' for granted can be ambiguous; that we can be looking at the same coin for example but have different perspectives; possibly because we are looking at different sides of the coin! In this scenario, it is easy to operate from a starting point of negative neutrality. It is in this light that it is essential for the reader to critically explore the construction of social reality and how this impacts on various people's experiences of globalisation, without being quick to dismiss other people's realities.

As globalisation is such a contested term, rooted in people's realities, it is important that we start, from this point, to factor in the multiple complexities involved in attaching 'human meaning making' to the emotions and responses globalisation provokes. As Scholte (2005) argues, the only consensus around globalisation is that it is contested.

Having argued in the last section that reality is often constructed from our 'own pair of spectacles', we will now go on to explore how the different perspectives of the debate on globalisation are presented. It is argued that:

> *Current debates about trade are dominated by ritualistic exchanges between two camps: the 'globaphiles' and the 'globaphobes'. 'Globaphiles' argue that trade is already making globalisation work for the poor. Their prescription for the future is 'more of the same'. 'Globaphobes' turn this world view on its head. They argue that trade is inherently bad for the poor. Participation in trade, so the argument runs, inevitably leads to more poverty and inequality. The corollary of this view is 'the less trade the better'.*

(Oxfam, 2002: 9)

Before we move further, let us pause for a minute and think about where we stand.

In the Global literacy continuum (Figure 2.1), the globaphiles are the proponents of globalisation, who can only see the good of globalisation whilst the globaphobes are the opponents of globalisation and cannot see any good in it. It is important to note that these positions of globaphiles and globaphobes are not fixed positions in totality but ways of understanding the various positions on globalisation. The middle ground might be described as global competence; this position can be said to describe those who are competent in understanding and situating their actions and reactions in a presently globalised world. It takes time and a lot of reflection to be globally competent, in the words of Freire (1972) gaining that critical consciousness to integrate reflection and action. So the reader should not worry if they are not there yet; the important thing at this juncture is to locate oneself in order to understand where one is, at the moment, and where one wants to be in the future; and what one needs to get there.

For some people, a lot of positives could be listed for globalisation, such as: the improvement of instantaneous communication in the different parts of the world, for example the involvement, even from a distance, with the Arab Spring of 2011 through Twitter and Facebook to overthrow despotic regimes;

the ability of business to expand; production and consumption of food from different parts of the world; and diffusion of Human Rights norms.

On the other hand, many critics can also point to many negative ways in which the process of globalisation has been used to create wanton destruction and wreak havoc on the livelihoods and environment of people in distant lands. Some of these people will point to the excesses of capitalism and growing inequality. You might take either of these two positions, but before you do, it is probably worth knowing that there are many possibilities on the global continuum and that it is not a choice exclusively between one or the other. In order to build on this view, it is important to consider at least two perspectives on the various reactions to globalisation. The ability to deliver effective Global Youth Work should be preceded by the development of critical literacy: to constantly reflect on our professional and personal values and on how our constructed social reality is constant motion, in influencing our actions and reactions. Please note that our position on the global continuum does not necessarily have to be fixed, it can slide either left or right as one comes across new information that supports the construction and deconstruction of realities.

Globaphiles, globaphobes and globacritics

Whilst the first two terms of this section's heading dominate the two extreme positions, it is however important to understand that there are many more varied reactions and interpretations to globalisation. Castells (1999, in Coronado, 2003: 10) presents three interpretations of how people react to the process of globalisation.

The first one is that of the 'globaphiles' who favour globalisation as a legitimising identity; Coronado sees legitimising identity as the way in which dominant institutions and structures legitimise, rationalise and normalise their reality, which is linked to the global neo-liberal project, and is a position of the globaphiles.

The second reaction is that of the 'globaphobes' who oppose globalisation as a 'resistance identity', and that of the critics of neo-liberal globalisation, who see globalisation as a project identity. The globaphobes, Coronado argues, have constructed a resistant ideology which is 'produced by those actors who are in a position/conditions of being devalued and/or stigmatised by the logic of domination' whose survival is 'entrenched in domination' (p. 9).

The third reaction to globalisation is that of the 'globacritics'; Coronado argues that this group has a project identity, which seeks to redefine their position in society and seeks overall structural transformation.

After reflecting on Coronado's thesis, let us consider Scholte (2005), which is explained in the following section.

Neoliberalism, rejectionism, reformism and transformism

Scholte (2005) identifies four main responses to globalisation, as in this section's heading. He argues that the neoliberals who believe in the concept of free and unregulated markets have used the opportunities of globalisation to trade unhindered and largely unrestricted on a world stage, with disastrous consequences for some parts of the world, based on the Washington Consensus.

> *According to neoliberalist tenets, globalisation should be approached with large-scale removal of official interventions in the market, especially through measures of liberalisation, deregulation, privatisation and fiscal constraint. This policy package has often been termed 'the Washington Consensus'.*

(Scholte, 2005: 10)

This view of neoliberalism has over time been presented as policy orthodoxy and is widely seen as 'common sense'. This is in contrast to the position of those Scholte classes as the rejectionists, who have come to the conclusion that globalisation is largely used as a vehicle for neo-liberalist projects with 'calamitous consequences'. 'For these critics, globality is by its very nature deeply and unacceptably unsafe, unjust, undemocratic and unsustainable' (Sholte, 2005: 41). He states that the rejectionists have gone to the extent of calling for 'de-globalisation' and are also called the anti-globalists. He further argues that:

> *Like rejectionists, reformists oppose neo-liberalist globalisation for inflicting major cultural, ecological, economic and psychological harms. However, in contrast to rejectionists, reformists affirm that a more global world is here to stay, and they seek to redirect globalization more positively on non-marketist lines.*

(p. 43)

Transformists, Scholte (2005) goes on to argue, do not necessarily seek to reform existing global structures of oppression; to the contrary, they propose radical changes that dismantle rationalism and capitalism.

These views offer us insights into a range of perceptions on and reactions to globalisation, and into whether people feel that it is a force for good or evil. What is significant to note at this juncture is that, as in the earlier discussion of constructed reality, whether globalisation is construed as a force for good or bad is in the eyes of the beholder, based on our individual experiences. What is most significant at this point, though, is the process of beginning to build our theory, based on our personal, professional and/or academic encounters. Global Youth Work, I would argue, is rooted in the pursuit of social justice, and this stance in itself is not value free; it is rooted in our construction of social reality, which again in itself is not neutral. Global Youth Work is also based on working with young people to deconstruct their reality to provoke what Freire (1972) calls critical consciousness. In order to support young people in this process of deconstructing their reality and normality, we must be secure in our own convictions and in where we stand on the global continuum. It is however important from the above exposition to note that three broad positions can be identified: those who support globalisation based on its neoliberal orientation, premised on the basis of a free market; those who oppose it on the same basis; and, in the middle, those who accept its potential but reject some of the ways it is used so far. Scholte (2005) calls those who hold this latter position 'reformist' and Coronado (2003) calls them 'globacritics'.

Conclusion

In this chapter, we have demonstrated that constructed reality is not a given but a dynamic process of dismantling and reconstructing 'human meaning making' on the basis of which the world is interacted with. We have also advanced our thesis of negative neutrality and the propensity of some practitioners to start operating from this basis, and its potential consequences. We have also explored the extreme positions of relativism and dogmatism and the need for global literacy and competence. Ultimately this chapter has illustrated that reactions to globalisation, by globaphiles, globaphobes and globacritics, are premised on experiential and spatial locations and this is the foundation on which effective Global Youth Work is based. This understanding of constructed reality will greatly influence Global Youth Work praxis.

References

Althusser, L. (1971) Ideology and Ideological State Apparatuses. In *Lenin and Philosophy and other Essays.* Althusser, L. (Ed.) New York: Monthly Review Press.

Berger, P. and Luckmann, T. (1966) *The Social Construction of Reality: A Treatise in the Sociology of Knowledge.* Harmondsworth: Penguin.

Boushel, M. (2000) What Kind of People Are We? 'Race', Anti-Racism and Social Welfare Research. *British Journal of Social Work,* 30: 71–89.

Coronado, J.P. (2003) Not 'Globaphiles' or 'Globaphobes', but 'Globacritics'. *Management of Social Transformations, Discussion Paper No. 66,* UNESCO.

Cunha, T. & Gomes, R. (2010). Against the Waste of Experiences in Intercultural Learning. In Ramberg, I. (Ed.) *Intercultural Learning in European Youth Work: Which Ways Forward?* Strasbourg: Council of Europe.

Davies, B. (2005) Youth Work: A Manifesto for our Times. *Youth and Policy*, 88.

Freire, P. (1972) *Pedagogy of the Oppressed*. Harmondsworth: Penguin.

Hoskins, B. & Sallah, M. (2011) Developing Intercultural Competence In Europe: The Challenges. *Language and Intercultural Communication*, 11: 2, 113–25.

Milanovic, B. (2006) Global Income Inequality: A review. *World Economics*, 7: 1, January-March.

Oakley, A. (1981) Interviewing Women: A Contradiction in Terms'. In Roberts, H. (Ed.) *Doing Feminist Research*. London: Routledge.

Otten, H. (2010) The Role of Intercultural Learning in European Youth Work. Ten theses – Yesterday and Today. In Ramberg, I. (Ed.) *Intercultural Learning in European Youth Work: Which Ways Forward?* Strasbourg: Council of Europe.

Oxfam (2002) *Rigged Rules and Double Standards: Trade, Globalisation, and the Fight against Poverty*. Great Britain: Oxfam.

Rogers, W.S. (1989) Childrearing in a Multicultural Society. In Rogers, W.S., Heavey, D. and Ash, E. (Eds.) *Child Abuse and Neglect: Facing The Challenge*. London: Batsford.

Said, E. (1998) Orientalism. In Rivkin, J. & Ryan, M.Cornwall (Eds.) *Literary Theory: An Anthology*. Oxford: Blackwell.

Sallah, M. (2008b) Global Youth Work: A Matter Beyond the Moral and Green Imperatives? In Sallah, M. & Cooper, S. (Eds.) *Global Youth Work: Taking it Personally*. Leicester: National Youth Agency.

Sallah, M. (2009b) Dawn of a New Europe: Addressing Otherness. In Sallah, M. and Howson, C. (Eds.) *Europe's Established and Emerging Immigrant Communities: Assimilation, Multiculturalism or Integration*. Stoke-on-Trent: Trentham.

Scholte, J. A. (2005) *Globalisation: A Critical Introduction*. Basingstoke: Palgrave

Solano, J. (2010) *Javier Solana calls for Europe to Play Role of 'World Governance Laboratory'* http://www.esade.edu/web/eng/about-esade/today/news/viewelement/142645/1/javier-solana-calls-for-europe-to-play-role-of-world-governance-laboratory. Accessed: 20th June 2010

Thompson, N. (2003) *Promoting Equality, Challenging Discrimination and Oppression*. Basingstoke: Palgrave Macmillan.

CHAPTER 3

Global Inequality

Introduction

In the previous two chapters, we have explored the many stances different people hold about globalisation; especially the multiple and sometimes conflicting perspectives from which reality is constructed. At the heart of the debate on globalisation, it can be argued, is the distribution of world resources and its accompanying consequences. The fundamental argument of those who oppose the present terms on which globalisation is conducted is their abhorrence of the use of the process of globalisation as an instrument to generate global inequality, to benefit a limited number of individuals at the gross disadvantage of the vast majority across the globe. Their view is a challenge to the normalisation of inequality and human suffering as being acceptable and merely regrettable. This inequality is manifested in two ways: the inequality that exists between countries and the inequality within countries. This is a significant issue that we need to explore in developing Global Youth Work practice and in fighting against social injustice. I have argued elsewhere (Sallah, 2008b) that the success of the West is based on the misery of the South, and that this is facilitated through structures that engender oppression and create global inequality. I would argue that the pursuit of social justice, in creating a more just world, implicitly or explicitly, is the fundamental principle that underpins Global Youth Work. Effective Global Youth Work must seek to reverse the entrenched trend of North/West – South domination and exploitation.

Objectives

1. Define inequality.
2. Understand the causes and consequences of inequality.
3. Explore the scale of global inequality.
4. Consider examples of inequality in our practice.
5. Explore the role of Bretton Woods institutions.
6. Explore the role of multinational and transnational corporations.

What is inequality?

Activity 1

- In groups, each participant will give an example of inequality.
- The group will choose the example that best illustrates inequality.
- The group also needs to make a link to the global.
- On the basis of the example chosen by each group, a definition will be advanced.

Comment

When we conceptualise inequality, for a lot of people it is often reduced to invisible statistics that are often difficult to contextualise, especially for those who have not been at the receiving end of its dark side. From the above exercise, key phrases to emerge might include 'power imbalance', 'oppression', 'unequal access', and these are significant in starting the process of deconstructing inequality. Thompson conceptualises oppression (2003) as being operated at the personal, cultural and structural levels; this work on anti-oppressive practice has been seminal in the social sciences. However I would like to point out that perhaps there is another dimension to the PCS model, the global, which deserves an increasingly significant place in the model; especially given the accelerated pace of globalisation and the increasing interconnectedness of our lives. In borrowing from Thompson's earlier work, I would like to conceptualise inequality as the disparity, the power imbalance that exists between individuals, communities, and nations on the basis of socially and biologically constructed differences linked to race, gender, sexuality, spatiality, nationality, neighbourhood, economic status and any other '-ism' that can be construed in the mind of man and woman. It is of cardinal significance that we highlight the structurally engineered nature of inequality in some instances and how this can be a deliberately constructed mechanism for the benefit of a few; I will illustrate this point later on in the chapter. I would further argue that these constructed differences are both cause and consequence of the construction and enacting of inequality. Inequality thus can be understood to incorporate political, economic, health and educational dimensions.

Global inequality

Having interacted with the dark side of global inequality from a very young age, I have grown up to be repulsed by its ugliness, and perhaps this is the reason why it is with great difficulty that I find academic objectivity – often constructed from Western middle and upper class perspectives – detached and quite often isolated from my reality and that of those who breathe the inequality fumes on a daily basis. I have breathed and lived the effects of man-made inequality, and cannot therefore start from minus two when it comes to the neutrality continuum (see Figure 2.2).

Two recent events shook me really badly, and I guess left me in tears. The first was in January 2012 when I went to a district in The Gambia with my students. Partly due to the poor rainy season, a leading NGO identified that over 90 per cent of the people living in the district were described as either poor or very poor, the majority falling in the latter category. Poor means not having more than one meal a day and the reader can imagine what very poor means. Over lunch with some of the affected people, one of the students asked them why things were the way they were and the oldest among the group said that 'it is an act of God and there is nothing we can do about it'.

The second incident was when I went to Nigeria in February 2012 to promote my institution and further its business interests. I lived in one of the most expensive hotels and consumed all the abundance Nigeria could provide and I was strongly encouraged to only leave the hotel when escorted. But by the third day, I got tired of it and decided to go for a jog on the beach five minutes away. Bearing in mind that I spent the first three days rubbing shoulders with parents, most of whom could afford to pay £8,000 annually for their children to attend 'A' level colleges in Nigeria, this was in sharp contrast to the squalor I encountered on the beach, with parents and children crawling from their makeshift cardboard houses and people defecating on the beach, as well as emaciated people touched by the hands of deprivation, visibly struggling, preparing yet again to hustle for whatever they could get, to just eke out survival for another day. I felt psychologically and physiologically sick for three days and three nights. I reflected on the fact that Nigeria has so much wealth and yet so much poverty. It is estimated that it has 167 million (Lawan, 2012) to 170 million people (Save the Children 2012), with some estimates putting 70.8 per cent of the population living on less than one dollar a day and 92.4 per cent on less than two dollars a day (UNDP, 2006). My heart also cried similarly in The Gambia. If we were to paint a social converse of this situation, it will show inequality as a given, constructed as a normality, as the old man's response to my students in The Gambia indicated. It will show that a small part of the earth's population consume most of the earth's resources; it will also show that this rat race has been constructed as normality and we are told that there is nothing we can do about it. This is global inequality, devoid of statistics. It is the logic of the system that we have succumbed to; to the contrary, I will continue to argue that it is an abomination.

Between country and within country inequality

In this chapter, I will be exploring two dimensions of inequality, between country inequality and within country inequality. Within country inequality points to the inequality that exists between the citizens of a particular country. To continue the earlier narrative, whilst I have seen massive deprivation and suffering in the Gambia, I have also seen affluence that knocks me breathless. This massive gap points to within-country inequality. Another clear illustration of this is in Brazil 'where the per capita income of the most affluent 10 per cent of the population is 32 times that of the poorest 40 percent' (UN 2005: 49). In this light, inequality should not be constructed on the simplistic notion of a North-South binary, but should contextualise the disparity that exists between citizens of a given country. Whilst we have highlighted the plight of the common Nigerian man or woman in terms of living on less than one or two dollars a day, there is also massive and unparalleled inequality in Nigeria, as alluded to in the spotlight on those able to pay £8,000 for their children to attend 'A' level colleges: 65 per cent of the national wealth is owned by 20 per cent of the population (Save the Children, 2012).

Similarly, whilst born and brought up in The Gambia, I have been residing in the UK for the past fourteen years at the time of writing this book, and again I have seen the standard of living in the UK in terms of health care, housing and welfare, to be much better than in The Gambia. This is called 'between country inequality'. To further illustrate this point, The Gambia's per capita income was $542 in 2009 compared with the UK's which stood at $35,238.7 in the same year. In relation to life expectancy from birth for the period 2010–2015, a female born in The Gambia is expected to live for 59.2 years whilst a male is expected to live for 55.7 years, in comparison to females born in the UK who can expect to live for 82.3 years and males 77.8 years. In relation to infant mortality rates, the figure, for the period 2010–2015 stood at 77.8 per 1,000 births in The Gambia and 4.5 per 1,000 for the UK in the same period (United Nations Statistics Division, online). These statistics illustrate the inequalities that exist between two countries and how babies born in either of these countries have their life chances and standards of living greatly affected by between country inequality. If we were to compare the Democratic Republic of Congo and France, we would see similarly huge disparities in socio-political and economic indicators: 'in 2006, the Democratic Republic of the Congo, a country with a population of approximately 57 million people, had a GDP per capita of $649. That same year, France, with a population of 60 million, recorded per capita income of $28,877' (Joyce, 2008: 1).

Global inequality can be conceptualised as 'redressing the balance between the wealthy and the poor' (UN, 2005: 1). In this economic conceptualisation of inequality, Milanovic (2006, 2007) offers three interpretations of global income inequality. His first concept of inequality examines the inequalities among countries' total incomes (their GDPs). This focuses on the income of individual countries in comparison to others without a consideration of the number of people in each country or the nature of income distribution within them. His second concept of income equality is where the countries' total income is divided by the countries' total population (the countries' per capita income). The third concept focuses on comparing income between world individuals.

Global inequality is beyond the economic dimension

From the above discourse, it is easy to conceptualise global inequality exclusively as income distribution; however global inequality has multiple dimensions beyond the economic face. The differences to people's access to education, health and even longevity of life are key differentials in measuring inequality. Inequality can be constructed beyond the traditional notions of income distribution, to incorporate inequalities in health, education and opportunities for socio-political participation (UN, 2005: 1).

In the 2005 UN report on the state of the world, non-economic indicators were identified as health, education, access to basic necessities (food, water, sanitation and housing) and opportunities for political participation (UN, 2005: 58).

> As non-economic aspects of inequality become more widely recognised, the distinctions that will inevitably be drawn between economic and non-economic inequality may create a false dichotomy between phenomena that are inextricably related. Inequality is complex and multidimensional and is manifested in various forms at the community, national and global levels. Individuals, groups and countries that lack opportunities at one level generally lack opportunities at other levels as well.
>
> (UN, 2005: 43)

As rightly emphasised in the above quote, although inequality has many dimensions, the different dimensions are interlinked and symbiotic and this will be given more space in the next chapter in relation to development. The economic wellbeing of a citizenry is deeply interconnected with the health and political freedoms of the citizenry, and this inextricability should be the departure point in highlighting the different dimensions of inequality.

Scale of global inequality

The scale and nature of global inequality must be understood before effective actions can be taken to redress the hubristic nature of those who spew and churn the neo-liberalistic line. The scale of inequality can be mind numbing and may lead to spasmodic fits of guilt and rage; guilt possibly for those who profit from an unfair global order and rage for those who survive on daily doses of hopelessness. Whatever the context of one's starting point, it is important to reflect on the following dimensions.

Economic dimension

Taking a critical look at global inequality will reveal some unpalatable truths, as has been argued:

> We find a world in which the top 20 percent of the population enjoys more than 70 percent of total income, contrasted by two paltry percentage points for those in the bottom quintile in 2007 under PPP-adjusted exchange rates; using market exchange rates, the richest population quintile gets 83 percent of global income with just a single percentage point for those in the poorest quintile.
>
> (Ortiz and Cummins, 2011: vii)

Ortiz and Cummins (2011: 11) further argue that 22 per cent of the world population have been living on less than $1.25 dollars a day and 40 per cent (2.2 billion) on less than $2 per day, in a world where 1 per cent of the world population had as much as 56 per cent of the world's population in 2007. In measuring inequality, many writers often speak of quintiles, which represent 20 per cent of the world population. Ortiz and Cummins (2011) estimate that 48.5 per cent are young people and are confined to the bottom two income quintiles. This means that out of the three billion persons under the age of 24 in the world as of 2007, approximately 1.5 billion were living in situations in which they and their families had access to just nine percent of global income. (Ortiz and Cummins, 2011: 12). The UN's Department of Economic and Social Affairs, in its report *The Inequality Predicament: Report on the World Social*

Situation, also highlighted that 80 per cent of the world's GDP is owned by 1 million living in the developed world whilst the world's 5 billion people living in the developing world own only 20 per cent of the world's GDP (UN, 2005: 1). These figures point to a massive disjuncture in the distribution of the earth's resources.

Health dimension of inequality

Over the last five years, life expectancy has increased worldwide from 47 to 65 years (UN, 2005). However this trend is reflected unequally. For example, if we are to look at child mortality, we will find that the child mortality rate for under fives was 176.9 per 1,000 births for Guinea in 1999, 219.9 for Burkina Faso in 1998/1999 and 229.1 for Mali in 2001. These numbers can be compared with 39 per 1,000 births in Armenia in 2000, 24.9 in Colombia in 2000 and 46.7 for Peru in 2000 (UN, 2005). These figures can further be sharply contrasted to 3 per 1,000 births in 2002 for Sweden, 4 for Denmark, 5 for Germany and 6 for Belgium. The huge difference, for example for children born in Mali in 1998/1999, where for every 1000 children born 229 will die before their fifth birthday, compared to three in every 1000 in Sweden, is no accident. Structures exist that make these ugly statistics possible. It is further worth noting that, 'of the 20 countries with the highest rates, 19 are in sub-Saharan Africa, the region that experienced the smallest decline (from 186 to 174 deaths per 1000 live births, or a reduction of only 2 percent) between 1990 and 2001' (UN, 2005: 65). We can go deeper into this scenario to highlight that:

> *Ninety-nine per cent of maternal deaths worldwide occur in developing countries, and in poor countries as many as 30 per cent of deaths amongst women of reproductive age (15–49 years) may be from pregnancy-related causes, compared with rates of less than 1 per cent for developed countries. In 2000, there were 400 maternal deaths per 100,000 live births in developing regions, a ratio 19 times higher than in developed regions.*
>
> (UN, 2005: 65)

This risk is 1 in 16 for sub-Saharan Africa compared to 1 in 4000 in Western Europe. What lessons can we draw here? That there is massive health inequality between countries in relation to child mortality and maternal deaths? These statistics only reflect two dimensions. We can continue to explore other dimensions: for example the death toll from malaria in sub-Saharan Africa is 1 million per annum, and it has a hand in the death of a further 2 million per annum. However, it is estimated that 90 per cent of all those who die from malaria live in sub-Saharan Africa, the vast majority of whom are children (UN 2005). Again, of the 852 million people estimated to be affected annually by malnutrition, 815 million live in developing countries, compared to 9 million in industrialised countries.

Malnutrition is one of the main causes of child mortality and accounts for 10.4 million children dying annually in the developing countries, given that 20 per cent of the total population in the developing world is malnourished (UN, 2005; Food and Agriculture Organisation, 2004). Additionally, developing countries lose an estimated US$500 billion every year due to hunger and malnutrition (Food and Agriculture Organisation, 2004).

We can go on and on to provide more information about education, hunger and malnutrition, housing, life expectancy and other dimensions of inequality; however the statistics will be similar to the ones quoted above. For example, whilst life expectancy has increased over the past 50 years from 47 to 65, the gap between the countries with the lowest and highest life expectancies stands at 36 years. If we are also to take a quick look at education, we might notice that whilst primary school net enrolment stood at 84 per cent globally in 2001, in North America and Western Europe it stood at over 90 per cent compared to 62.8 per cent in sub-Saharan Africa (UN, 2005). These statistics establish that inequality exists, that it is nauseating and at times unbelievable, but that these are the conditions that some of us have come to accept as normal. The fundamental thesis which I will continue to advance throughout this book is that this status is not necessarily an act of God, as the old man told my students, but results from man-made conditions which grossly disadvantage one group over another. This 'seductive logic' needs challenging.

Overhauling global inequality at a snail's pace

The disproportionate nature of world inequality is not only widespread, entrenched and pervasive, it is also being overhauled at a snail's pace; the poorest 40 per cent of the world population, between 1990 and 2007, only increased its share of global income by 1 per cent (Ortiz and Cummins, 2011: 2). Ortiz and Cummins further argue that:

> . . . it took 17 years for the bottom billion to improve their share of world income by 0.18 percentage points, from 0.77 percent in 1990 to 0.95 percent in 2007. At this speed, it would take more than eight centuries (855 years to be exact) for the bottom billion to have ten percent of global income.

(Ortiz and Cummins, 2011: 10)

The UN report on the world social situation (UN, 2005) notes that there was a decline between 1981 and 2001 in the proportion of the world's population living in extreme poverty from 40 per cent to 21 per cent. However this figure overall does not reveal the true nature of the poverty that huge parts of the world continue to experience, especially given the huge strides made by the Asian giants (China and India) who constitute almost 40 per cent of the world's population (UN, 2005: 2). Whilst there has been a huge decline in poverty, the bulk of this, it can be argued, has not been evenly distributed and is represented in the strides of China and India. This figure overall dropped from 1.2 to 1.1 billion, but the Chinese and Indian figures mask these figures. Between 1981 and 2001, the number of people living on less than $2 a day in China fell from 88 per cent to 47 per cent, and the number of people living on less than $1 per day dropped from 634 million to 212 million. In the same vein, the number of those living in India on less than £2 a day fell from 90 per cent to 80 per cent (UN, 2005). On the other hand, in sub-Saharan Africa, the number of the poor increased by 90 million in the same period.

Consequences of global inequality

Ortiz and Cummins (2011) argue that income inequality is dysfunctional and leads to slow economic growth, results in health and social problems, generates political instability and aggravates social inequalities especially in relation to children. As has been incisively argued, the:

> . . . failure to address this inequality predicament will ensure that social justice and better living conditions for all people remain elusive, and that communities, countries and regions remain vulnerable to social, political and economic upheaval.
>
> (UN, 2005: 1)

Not only will inequality breed present consequences, it also has the potential for the intergenerational transmission of poverty and all its attendant consequences. It has the potential to ignite civil strife (Sen, 1997). In fact may I be so bold as to suggest that most major revolutions have been caused by inequality: for example Mohamed Bouazizi's rage leading to his self-immolation triggered the Tunisian revolution, and some might even ague, the Arab Spring; this act was encapsulated in an acute act of injustice and inequality. Given the increasing interconnectedness of the world, the heightened potential must be recognised. Inequality impacts on growth as it limits educational attainment and human capital development, as well as brewing social tensions which also impact on economic activity (UN, 2005; Cornia and Court, 2001).

The nature of inequality is grotesque and for some it provokes an urge to throw up. The realisation of the true scale and nature of global inequality can lead to temporary paralysis, leading to a feeling of guilt: consequently some would rather bury their head in the sand and hear no evil and see no evil, but this would not make it go away. To the contrary, it will be aggravated, more virulent and still be there when we open our eyes!

Ways of measuring global inequality

To measure global inequality is an almost impossible task as no two contexts are the same, especially in relation to validity and reliability. However, attempts have been put in place to establish some element of measurability when it comes to inequality and poverty. Some of these measurement tools are set out below.

GDP per capita

This is the total market value of all goods and services produced within a country, divided by the average number of citizens. Whilst this method of measurement is good at giving an idea of a country's wealth, it does not necessarily give the true picture in a given country as it can sometimes fail to highlight within country inequality as well as great pockets of deprivation and poverty. This measurement is based on the principle of mean averages and therefore does not necessarily recognise the uneven distribution of wealth; additionally, it does not necessarily incorporate other non-economic dimensions of inequality.

Gini co-efficient

The Gini index is a measurement of the distribution of individual/household income or consumption expenditure in comparison to a perfect distribution. The Lorenz Curve is used to plot the total income received against the number of recipients: 0 is perfect equality and 1 is perfect inequality. Whilst this is a widely used method of measuring inequality, some social scientists avoid it due to the difficulty of establishing context when it comes to how income is counted in different countries; others avoid it through being not very familiar with statistical calculations.

Human Development Index

The Human Development Index (HDI) was first introduced in the 1990 UNDP *Human Development Report* and has now become a main feature of their annual Human Development Report that focuses on measuring development and by extension, inequality. The significance of this approach to measurement is its recognition of the non-economic dimensions of inequality. Unlike the GDP per capita and the Gini co-efficient, which mainly focus on income and its distribution as the main facets, the Human Development Index incorporates the three main dimensions of health, education and living standards, and the four indicators of life expectancy at birth, mean years of schooling, expected years of schooling and gross national income per capita. This method creates a more rounded approach to measuring quality of life and inequality. Some critics argue that the use of averages, as in the two earlier cited measurement tools, hide huge pockets of disparities (Foster et al., 2005; Seth, 2009). For a more detailed exploration of the critique against the HDI, please explore Kovacevic (2011).

Causes of global inequality

A fundamental question that I find practitioners grappling with, as well as during my reflection in practice, is the question of why things are the way they are. Why is it that in the abundance of this earth, 80 per cent of the world's resources are consumed by 20 per cent of the world's population? There are far too many reasons to go into: however, I will contend that a key stumbling block to equality is the present economic arrangement that dominates the world, clearly manifested in the Bretton Woods Institutions set-up and the receding powers of the state juxtaposed to the ascendency of the Multinational/Transnational corporations, with accompanying gravitas. As it has been pointed out:

> *Macroeconomic and trade liberalization policies, economic and financial globaliz-ation, and changes in labour market institutions cannot be disconnected from the struggle to achieve social development, equality and social justice. The failure to pursue a comprehensive, integrated approach to development will perpetuate the inequality predicament, for which everyone pays the price.*
>
> (UN, 2005: 7)

A dysfunctional economic system permeates the world, one that has seen the corporate manufacture of inequality, largely guided by the dictum of profit, regardless of the cost to others. Two main dominant forces vied for domination until the late 1980s, when the collapse of the Berlin Wall elevated the market economy approach as the dominant mainstay. As argued in the previous chapters, the acceleration of the process of globalisation has made it possible for Multinational and Transnational corporations to trade, unhindered and instantaneously, across the globe. This has led to the satisfaction of share-holders being seen as the key objective in trading. This has also seen the receding of the traditional powers of the state: whilst the traditional powers of the state contract and become less effectual in influencing the lives of its traditionally spatially bounded citizenry, the TNCs/MNCs have become more powerful in determining and impacting on the lives of citizens, across states and boundaries in an era of conquered space and time. Let us for a moment distinguish between MNCs and TNCs before exploring the role of the Bretton Woods Institutions.

TNCs and MNCs

Multinational Corporations (MNCs) are entities operating in more than one country through branches and subsidiaries, whilst Transnational/Transglobal Corporations are mostly 'enterprises that have largely severed relevant connections with their home nation-states and operate disregarding the interests and well-being of the home country to a significant degree' (Bonanno, and Antonio, online).

In giving evidence to the House of Lords Select Committee on Economic Affairs, Christian Aid, postulated that:

> . . . over the last 30 years, the number and size of TNCs has increased dramatically. In 1970, there were 7,000 TNCs, whilst today there are 63,000 parent companies operating with about 690,000 subsidiaries in almost all sectors, countries, industries and economic activities in the world.
>
> (House of Lords Select Committee on Economic Affairs, 2002)

It was also asserted in the report that 'many TNCs are bigger than most countries in which they operate. In 1998, the annual turnover of BP was larger than the GDP of all the least developed countries combined'. Two main concerns were raised in this light. The first is linked to the democratic deficit where TNCs/MNCs are able to wield and effect considerable influence at the national and international levels; without being answerable to the general population, instead they owe their allegiance to a small number of stake-holders, whose foremost desire is profit. Linked to this first concern is 'the consequence of the exercise of that power on employment standards, the capacity of governments to pursue social welfare programmes, on the environment and culture' (House of Lords Select Committee on Economic Affairs, 2002). The concern here is that because TNCs and MNCs are not accountable to anyone but their shareholders, they are able to invest mobile stateless capital, aided by the process of globalisation, to any corner of the world wherever that be, as long as it can return the hugest amount of profit in the shortest possible time; and this, the charge sheet goes, has continued to lead to the entrenchment of inequality in the most vulnerable parts of the world.

Bretton Woods Institutions

The Bretton Woods Conference (United Nations Monetary and Financial Conference) brought together representatives from 44 nations from 1–22 July, 1944 in Bretton Woods, New Hampshire. The Bretton Woods Institutions are made up of three main components: the International Monetary Fund (IMF), the World Bank and the World Trade Organisation (formerly the General Agreement on Tariffs and Trade). The IMF is charged with overseeing currency values and acts as 'credit union'. It also polices countries' macroeconomic policies and controls based on conditionalities. The World Bank is made up of the following components:

- International Bank for Reconstruction and Development
- International Finance Corporation
- International Development Association
- International Centre for the Settlement of Disputes
- Multilateral Guarantee Investment Agency

The World Trade Organisation was born in 1995 to replace GATT, and its main purpose is to make sure that governments keep within agreed limits; it also emphasises that international trade agreements should supersede national economic policies. These three major organs who make up the Bretton Woods Institutions have been under considerable fire for some time, often charged with providing the legal framework, and acting as a blunt instrument, to consciously or unconsciously engrain inequality. This criticism has been widely levelled against it, from its governance to its use of resources (Woods, N. 2006; Leech, D. & Leech, R., 2003).

Power, control and impact

The governance of the Bretton Woods Institutions has come under severe criticism because their power, control and impact have far-reaching conse-quences, especially for those who bear witness to the worst excesses of global inequality. It is worth noting that the G8 controlled 48.18 per cent of votes in the IMF and 45.71 per cent of the World Bank (New Internationalist, March

2004). At the Hong Kong World Trade Organisation Summit, the EU had 832 delegates, the US 356, Japan 229, Bolivia 7, Burundi 3, Gambia 2 and Central African Republic 0 (New Internationalist, April 2006). This further illustrates the inequality of representation, and by extension, the inequality of influence and the exercise of socio-economic interest where the key decisions are being made in terms of global trade arrangements.

It is equally crucial to highlight that in 2000, the Joint Economic Committee of the US Congress found a failure rate of 55–60 per cent for all World Bank-sponsored projects; in Africa, the failure rate reached 73 per cent. These mechanisms, exemplified by the Bretton Woods Institutions, illustrate how the manufacture of global inequality is maintained and sustained by systemic failings from an entity that was meant to address the very problems it now stands accused of exacerbating. To this end, it should not come as a surprise that for every dollar in grant aid to developing countries, more than 13 come back in debt repayments. It was also estimated in 2005 that developing countries were losing as much as $700 billion annually due to trade barriers (Seen Environmental Learning, online), mostly put in place or facilitated by the Bretton Woods Institutions.

Destructive Bretton Woods policies

Whilst the Bretton Woods Institutions were set up in the aftermath of the Second World War to facilitate trade between nations, support development projects by providing loans, and negotiate rules and standards for international trade (Madeley et al. 1994), the core of its purpose continues to be questioned and these institutions have become the focus of vitriolic protestations, as enumerated in Chapter 1. For some, these institutions have become everything that is wrong with globalisation based on a neo-liberal agenda which seeks to reduce the role of governments in the economy, promote private sector operations, eliminate restrictions in the economy, and ensure market determined prices (Skosireva and Holaday, 2010: 75; Easterly, 2007). These interventions include Structural Adjustment Policies (SAP), the Programme for Sustained Development (PSD), and the Economic Recovery Programme (ERP). As highlighted in the following quote:

> *The process of globalization, particularly in developing countries, has been signifi-*
> *cantly accelerated through the global economic policies implemented by major*
> *international financial institutions such as the International Monetary Fund and the*
> *World Bank. While the primary goal of these neoliberal policies was geared towards*

financial stability and economic development, there (is) evidence of negative impacts of these policies on the health of the population in the countries of the third world.

(Skosireva and Holaday, 2010: 73)

It is significant to note that 'from 3 per cent of total World Bank lending in 1981, structural adjustment credits rose to 19 per cent in 1986. Five years later, the figure was 25 per cent' (Chowdhury, 2012: 87). According to Oxfam:

> *Powerful transnational companies (TNCs) have been left free to engage in investment and employment practices which contribute to poverty and insecurity, unencumbered by anything other than weak voluntary guidelines. The World Trade Organisation (WTO) is another part of the problem. Many of its rules on intellectual property, investment, and services protect the interests of rich countries and powerful TNCs, while imposing huge costs on developing countries. The WTO's bias in favour of the self-interest of rich countries and big corporations raises fundamental questions about its legitimacy.*

(Oxfam, 2002: 4)

These concerns highlight the perceived ineffectiveness of Bretton Woods interventions in dismantling the structures that promote global inequality. If the very structures that are supposed to liberate, oppress, then how do we promote an alternative to the orthodoxy?

Trade barriers

In 2000, more than 50 per cent of Asia's exports, 75 per cent of Latin America's exports, and 70 per cent of Africa's exports of merchandise goods were destined for Western Europe, North America, or Japan (WTO, 2001). Given this high level of dependency on exports, especially exports to Western Europe and North America, where the rules of the game are 'rigged' (Oxfam, 2002) and where the only possible outcome is the growth of inequality in developing countries, how do we arrest a system that is only capable of generating inequality and disadvantage? The problem, as Oxfam highlights, is not the inability of countries to develop and generate an acceptable living standard for its citizens; it is in effect a destructive and exploitative system of world domination whose foundation was laid during the era of slavery and colonialism, with the sole purpose of serving Western markets, regardless of the consequences:

> *If developing countries increased their share of world exports by just five per cent, this would generate $350bn – seven times as much as they receive in aid. The $70bn that Africa would generate through a one per cent increase in its share of world*

exports is approximately five times the amount provided to the region through aid and debt relief.

(Oxfam, 2002: 8)

The 48 least-developed countries (LDCs) face tariffs on average 20 per cent higher than the rest of the world on their exports to industrialised countries. This rises to 30 per cent higher for manufacturing exports (IMF and World Bank, 2001). As highlighted in the Oxfam report, 'LDCs are losing an estimated $2.5bn a year in potential export earnings as a result of the high levels of tariff protection in Canada, the EU, Japan, and the United States' (Oxfam, 2002: 101). In addition to these tariff barriers, there are also the non-tariff barriers (import quotas, product standards) which according to Oxfam, raise the level of protection afforded to European industries from 5.1 per cent to 9 per cent if both tariff and non-tariff barriers are included (Oxfam, 2002).

Anti-dumping measures (where a country sells its products abroad for less than it would charge at home, or for less than the cost of production) have been used in a way it is easy to feel scathing about. Since the WTO agreement was signed in 1995, it is significant to observe that the EU and USA have initiated 234 anti-dumping actions against developing countries. It is also imperative to be aware, in relation to tariffs, of the disproportionate and disabling nature of their application: 'the EU applies a 250 per cent tariff on imported meat products, and the USA and Canada impose import tariffs exceeding 120 per cent on groundnuts and meat products respectively' (Oxfam, 2002: 102).

Conclusion

In this chapter, we started with the definition of inequality and then delved deeper to explore global inequality. We also explored within country and between country inequalities and argued that economic inequality is only one of many dimensions of inequality, in addition to health, education and access to nutrition. We further argued that global inequality is grotesque, and a demonstration of its scale and nature can be nauseating; and the sad fact remains that the reversal of this trend is only moving a snail's pace. We investigated some of the ways of measuring global inequality but came to the conclusion that the three methodological approaches we explored have inherent deficits as no two contexts of inequality are the same; however whilst reliability and validity of these methodological choices might be questioned, they do provide us with instruments to gauge the scale and nature of inequality globally. We concluded by discussing two structural causes of inequality at the global level, namely the role of Bretton Woods Institutions and TNCs/MNCs, in entrenching inequality

Based on the above discourse, it is possible to observe how the structures that engender inequality are sewn into the very fabric of a global order premised on the Washington Consensus; these structural measures enable the focus on capital and profit, which permeates and seeps into the local and global psyche. How much farmers can get for their agricultural and poultry productions is largely influenced by the trade barriers that North American and Western European governments have put in place and this again is inextricably linked to the local and national economies of developing countries, and ultimately to survival at the personal level there.

As a youth worker who has practiced both in the South and in the North, I have observed that this contextualisation is often missing from our analysis. To facilitate change, we have to address it from two separate, but symbiotically linked, angles: the personal/interpersonal and the political/structural. In my practice of over 20 years as a youth worker, I have often observed that youth and community workers have a good grasp of the personal and interpersonal: what the issues are in a given community, individually and collectively, and how they can mutually engage the community towards addressing their learning and development needs; but they might not engage with the political and structural, as their fixation is with the personal–local and some might not even be interested in the structural. These youth and community workers might be able to mobilise communities, and support them to take action, which does quite well in the personal/interpersonal, however the structural forces of oppression remain, and might even become more virulent, once poked in the tail.

On the other hand, a number of organisations work at the structural level, and bring about structural change without the grassroots signing up to be custodians of such changes. Whilst this is good in many ways, there is scant ownership by those most affected by these developments, and therefore very few will rise up to defend it when these structural changes are being eroded.

A simultaneous assault on the personal/interpersonal and the political/structural is therefore needed, one which understands the structural causes of global inequality as well as one which starts and links these sometimes distant inequalities to the personal and interpersonal at the local and international levels. How is the livelihood of a farmer in a remote part of Gambia linked to the trade barriers erected in Western Europe or North America? To challenge global inequality, then, requires a critical understanding of the causes, consequences and scale of inequality both at the local and global levels; it also requires action at both the personal/interpersonal and political/structural levels. Disjointed action will lead to a lack of constructive alignment (Biggs, 1999).

References

Biggs, J. (1999) *Teaching for Quality Learning at University: What the Student Does. 1st Edition*. Buckingham: SRHE/Open University Press.

Bonanno, A. and Antonio, R. (2012, online) *Multinational Corporations*. Wiley-Blackwell Encyclopaedia of Globalization http://onlinelibrary.wiley.com/doi/10.1002/9780470670590.wbeog408/abstract;jsessionid=B4AF76F2FB94A6D2C96A5004A7E18DFC.f03t02

Chowdhury, A. (2012) Structural Adjustment and Crises: Which Way Now? *Institutions and Economies*, 4: 1, 85–118.

Cornia, G.A. and Court, J. (2001) *Inequality, Growth and Poverty in the Era of Liberalization and Globalization*. UNU World Institute for Development Economics Research. Finland: UNU/WIDER.

Easterly, W. (2007) Was Development Assistance a Mistake? *American Economic Review*, 97: 2, 328–32.

Food and Agriculture Organisation of the United Nations (2004) *The State of Food Insecurity in the World: Monitoring Progress Towards the World Food Summit and Millennium Development Goals*. Rome: FAO.

Foster, J.E., Lopez-Calva, L. and Szekely, M. (2005). Measuring the Distribution of Human Development: Methodology and an Application to Mexico. *Journal of Human Development*, 6: 1, 5–29.

House of Lords Select Committee on Economic Affairs (2002) *Globalisation*. http://www.publications.parliament.uk/pa/ld200203/ldselect/ldeconaf/5/507.htm

IMF and World Bank (2001) *Market Access for Developing Countries Exports*. Washington: International Monetary Fund/World Bank.

Joyce, J. (2008) Globalization and Inequality Among Nations. forthcoming in Sisay Asefa (Ed.) *Globalization and International Development*. Kalamazoo, MI: W.E. Upjohn Institute.

Kovacevic, M. (2011) *Human Development Research Paper 2010/33 Review of HDI Critiques and Potential Improvements*. UNDP.

Lawan, M.M. (2012) *Statement of The Senate Chairman, Committe on Population on 7 Billion World Population Day*. http://www.population.gov.ng/index.php/publications/84-news/latest/109-statement-of-the-senate-chairman-committe-on-population-on-7-billion-world-population-day

Leech, D. & Leech, R. (2003) *Voting Power in the Bretton Woods Institutions*. Paper presented to the Development Studies Association Conference, Glasgow, 10–12th September.

Madeley, J., Sullivan, D. and Woodroffe, J. (1994) *Who Runs the World?* London: Christian Aid.

Milanovic, B. (2006) Global Income Inequality: A Review. *World Economics*, 7: 1, January–March.

Milanovic, B. (2007) Globalization and Inequality. In Held, D. and Kaya, A. (Eds.) *Global Inequality*. Polity Press: Cambridge.

New Internationalist Issue 388, April (2006)

New Internationalist, Issue 365 March (2004)

Ortiz, I. and Cummins, M. (2011) *Global Inequality: Beyond The Bottom Billion*. Social and Economic Policy Working Paper, New York: UNICEF.

Oxfam (2002) *Rigged Rules and Double Standards: Trade, Globalisation, and The Fight Against Poverty*. Oxfam.

Sallah, M. (2008b) Global Youth Work: A Matter Beyond the Moral and Green Imperatives? In: *Global Youth Work: Taking it Personally.* (Eds.) Sallah, M. and Cooper, S. Leicester: National Youth Agency.

Save the Children (2012) *Born Equal: Country Case Study: Nigeria.* http://www.savethechildren.org.uk/sites/default/files/images/Born_Equal_Nigeria_case_study.pdf

Seen Environmental Learning, online http://www.nied.edu.na/divisions/projects/SEEN/SEEN%20 Publications/Environmental%20Information%20Sheets/Globalisation/5.%20Debt, aid%20and%20en vironment.pdf

Sen, A. (1997) *On Economic Inequality.* Oxford: Oxford University Press.

Seth, S. (2009) Inequality, Interactions, and Human Development. *Journal of Human Development and Capabilities*, 10, 375–96.

Skosireva, A.K. and Holaday, B. (2010) Revisiting Structural Adjustment Programs in Sub-Saharan Africa: A Long-Lasting Impact on Child Health. *World Medical & Health Policy*, 2: 3, Article 5.

Thompson, N. (2003) *Promoting Equality, Challenging Discrimination and Oppression.* Basingstoke: Palgrave Macmillan.

UN Data (online) *Country Profile: Gambia.* http://data.un.org/CountryProfile.aspx?crName= Gambia

UN Department of Economic and Social Affairs (2005) *The Inequality Predicament.* Report on the World Social Situation. New York: United Nations.

UNDP (2006) *Beyond Scarcity: Power, Poverty and The Global Water Crisis.* Human Development Report. New York: UNDP.

United Nations Statistics Division (online)

Woods, N. (2006) Bretton Woods Institutions. In Weiss, T.G. and Daws, S. (Eds.) *Oxford Handbook on the United Nations.* Oxford: Oxford University Press.

WTO (2001) *International Trade Statistics.* Geneva: WTO.

CHAPTER 4

Sustainable Development

Introduction

In the previous chapter, we explored the grotesque and pervasive nature of global inequality both between and within countries as well as the structural mechanisms in place to oversee the status quo. A key emerging narrative is the need to dismantle an unsustainable and inequitable system that greatly disadvantages one group over another. Whilst this might not be a universal position, in fact some academic postulations might vehemently contradict it, I speak from a social justice position with an acute understanding of the contestability of my position; I unashamedly state this position from the outset. Given that I am proposing something different and more sustainable, what am I suggesting?

In this chapter, I intend to explore notions of development and sustainability and how, in attempting to deconstruct a seductive logic, we can advance different models of development that are counter to the orthodoxy explored in the last chapter. Global Youth Work, I will argue in the next chapter (Chapter 5), should be immersed in fighting for social justice, in an explicitly political stance. Anything short of this, in my opinion, equates to applying balm only to soothe the conscience, suffering from a daily exposure to the mind numbing illogicality of global inequality; but not to addressing systemic failings.

In advancing an alternative thesis of development, it is pivotal that we engage with current perspectives of development, and with how we can engrain the concept of sustainability as a key component in our praxis. It is also important to state from the outset that sustainable development is not only limited to the environmental imperative; significantly it must be cognisant of the political, social, economic and health infrastructures that imbue human socialisation and existence. This interconnectedness, for example, is shown in the symbiotic relationship between education, health, employment and sustainable govern-ance structures, and how they are inextricably linked to one another.

Objectives

1. Introduce the concept of development and sustainable development.
2. Explore the different dimensions of sustainable development.

3. Explore the interconnectedness and reciprocity of development in a globalised world.
4. Explore key milestones in the sustainable development discourse.

What is development?

As discussed in the last chapter, an attendant consequence of global inequality is the unequal distribution of the earth's resources, a growing divide between the haves and the have-nots, and unnecessary and grotesque human suffering, to a large extent maintained by structural violence. In the context of Global Youth Work, sustainable development seeks to promote an understanding of development, to study the causes of underdevelopment and to support communities to empower themselves to promote their own development. In starting this chapter, it is pertinent that we explore exactly what is meant by development. According to the Human Development report:

> *Human development is the expansion of people's freedoms to live long, healthy and creative lives; to advance other goals they have reason to value; and to engage actively in shaping development **equitably and sustainably on a shared planet**. People are both the beneficiaries and the drivers of human development, as individuals and in groups.*

(UNDP 2010: 2)

The above definition highlights the significance of people's freedoms in living healthy, long and fulfilled lives in the pursuit of happiness; it represents a progression from one perceived state to a better one. However, this is one of many philosophical stances underpinning the notion of development postulated by the UNDP, Sen (1993, 1999b, 2005) Haq (1995) and others of such persuasion; the very concept of development and what it encapsulates is a site of contestation: is it synonymous with consumerist and materialistic conceptions of growth? Is it the same as Westernisation or in line with attempts to 'de-westernise' development theory? Is the neoclassical, modernisation, dependency/structuralist/post-development or earlier mentioned human development approach the right approach to development? Is development all about economics?

Pieterse (2009: 9) offers a number of perspectives of development over time, ranging from the 1800s with the Classical political economy/Late-comers who focused on finding remedies for progress and catching up with more advanced nations, mainly through industrialisation. He highlights the period from 1940 as Development economics, with a focus on economic growth and industrialisation; the 1950s as Modernisation, with a focus on social and economic growth; and the 1960s as Dependency theory where largely Southern countries sought to refocus development interventions by what he terms 'autocentric' approaches to development. The 1980s, he argues, were the era of Human Development approaches, as contained in the work of Sen (in Pieterse, 2009) which focused on 'Capacitation' and 'enlargement of people's choices'; another development model perpetuated in the 1980s, he argues, was the Neo-liberal model with a focus on 'structural reform', deregulation, liberalization, privatisation'. He highlights Post-development in the 1990s with a focus on 'Authoritarian engineering' and Millennium Development Goals in 2000 with a focus on Structural reforms. However, he concludes that 'development thinking and policy, then, is a terrain of hegemony and counter hegemony. In this contestation of interests there are many stakeholders and multiple centres of power and influence' (Pieterse, 2009: 9). Given the multifaceted conceptual-isations of development and the whole gambit of interpretation it is subjected to, we do not intend to give conclusive definitions of development, as that is beyond the scope of this chapter. However, we would like to explore some thinking behind some of the cardinal contours informing the development terrain. Whilst not exhaustive by any stretch of the imagination, the following section introduces different perspectives for those new to development theory.

Modernisation

Development has often been seen as modernisation and premised on the ideal of westernisation; industrialisation was seen as a key component of this (Elliot, 2013). However, an understanding of development should be premised on a multi-dimensional appreciation of human, social and natural capital; and perhaps sustainable development must incorporate all three.

Rostow's *Stages of Economic Growth* (1960) perhaps best explains Modern-isation, epitomising the linear-stages-of-growth model, as a theory of develop-ment. He conceives of development as a five stage process: a technologically limited static society which he sees as a traditional society; commercial exploitation of agriculture and extractive industry as preconditions for take-off; development of a manufacturing sector as the take-off phrase; development of a wider industrial and commercial base as the drive to maturity; develop-ment of welfare services resulting in high mass consumption, at which point a society is said to be developed. Daly and Regan (2012) highlight a number of criticisms against Rostow's (1960) thesis, principally that the contextual location of his theory is based on a limited sample of Western countries which is inappropriate and inapplicable to a significant number of other countries; additionally the theory fails to incorporate historical experiences of colonialism and imperialism. Another point made was that not all societies aspire for high mass consumption as an apex of development.

Structuralism/dependency theory

Whilst both structuralism and dependency theory have been born out of the concern that Western development paradigms have been unable to understand, even less deal with, the *situatedness* of Southern countries and their development needs, the solution they propose exhibits some divergence, with dependency theory being more radical in its approach. 'While structuralism argued in favour of an inward-directed development policy largely through import-substituting industrialisation (ISI), dependency theory proposed a new international economic order and, in one of its strands, a transition to socialism as a way out of underdevelopment' (Kay and Gwynne, 2000: 50). In the Radical/Dependency school of thought of development, it is said that:

> The assertion in dependency theory was that underdevelopment was not the result of any inadequacies in economic, social or environmental conditions within those countries themselves, but the direct outcome of development elsewhere and the manner in which those countries were incorporated into the operations of the international capitalist system, that is, the structural disadvantages of these countries and regions.
>
> (Elliot, 2013: 29)

Dependency theories of development emerged post-1945 as a critique of and protest against Westernisation and capitalist hegemony.

> Dependency theorists also argued that the development of young or emerging economies requires their withdrawal from the structure of exploitation that existed worldwide and in many cases the adoption of socialism rather than capitalism. Since capitalism was inextricably intertwined with colonialism and imperialism, then anti-colonialism needed to adopt socialism.
>
> (Elliot, 2013: 41)

Consequently the concept of Import Substitute Industrialisation as a strategy was developed by proponents of the dependency school of development largely in Latin America (for example see Escobar, 1995). This approach to development sought to refocus on developing domestic industries to serve domestic consumption. These approaches to development highlight the need for strong state intervention and to some extent the enacting of protectionist policies.

Neo-classical/Neo-liberal

The Neo-classical model of development saw a resurgence in the 1980s, and sees the role of the state as facilitating economic growth by creating a conducive environment for businesses to operate in, and not in instituting protectionist and restrictive conditions that impede the flow of the market. Premised on labour, capital and technology, this model of development is based on the 'Washington Consensus' of deregulation and opening up of markets; its answer to critics in the developing world is that government intervention and restrictionism would only result in inefficiency and snuff out the creative potential of markets. The 2008 financial crises, with its origins in the sub-prime mortgage in the US, has seen increasing state interventions even in that market, for example through quantitative easing and other such measures to save the market from crashing, and therefore begs the question as to whether the state can remain neutral in market affairs.

Human Development

The Human Development approach, as contained in the work of Amartya Sen (1993, 1999b, 2005) and Malibul Al Haq (1995), two of the best known proponents, and in the Human Development reports annually produced since 1990 by the UNDP, attempts to shift development from the economy as primary to human beings as the centre of development intervention. It debunks the notion that economic development will 'trickle down'.

As noted by Crocker (1992, 1995 in Stanton 2007) an important observation about the shift in focus introduced by the Human Development approach is as follows:

> *Amartya Sen and Martha Nussbaum are together credited with the origination of the 'capabilities' approach to human well-being based on Rawlsian philosophy (Pattanaik, 1994). Like Aristotle, Sen and Nussbaum focused attention on what human beings can do, instead of on what they have. Moving the discussion away from utility and towards 'capabilities' allowed Sen and Nussbaum to distinguish means (like money) from ends (like well-being or freedom).*
>
> (Stanton 2007: 9)

Sen's (1999a) capabilities approach emphasises human wellbeing and standard of living over the traditional economic measurements like per capita income. Stanton (2007) postulates that whilst Sen could not be tempted to identify what he thought these human capabilities are, as his position is that they need to be negotiated democratically, Nussbaum (2000) on the other hand has proposed a list of ten capabilities: (1) life (2) bodily health (3) bodily integrity (4) senses, imagination, and thought (5) emotions (6) practical reason (7) affiliation (8) other species (9) play, and (10) control over one's environment (Stanton, 2007).

Post-development

Voices from the 'post-development' school claim that, at best, development has failed, or at worst it was always a 'hoax', designed to cover up violent damage being done to the so-called 'developing' world and its people.

(Thomas, 2000: 3)

Champions of the post-development school of thought often argue that the western model of development as a panacea has not worked for those in the third word and has remained an elusive dream that is unattainable; to this end, the present western influenced paradigms of development must be discarded, to be replaced by new configurations of conceptualising and operationalising development. According to Elliot (2013: 37), 'a post-development era depends on breaking the "holds of westernisation", be it as organised by the aid industry or by the activities of western private capital.' Post-development theory does not seek to produce alternative versions of development; on the contrary, it advocates a complete overhaul of current development paradigms and instead calls for the establishment of development alternatives (Escobar 1992, 1995, 2000; Rahnema 1997). It is premised on the foundations that:

. . . the idea of development stands like a ruin in the intellectual landscape. Delusion and disappointment, failures and crimes have been the steady companions of development and they tell a common story: it did not work.

(Sachs, 1992: 1)

Perhaps one of the best best known exponents of this school of thought exposes this most succinctly:

. . . they are interested not in development alternatives but in alternatives to development . . . an interest in local culture and knowledge; a critical stance towards established scientific discourses; and the defence and promotion of localised, pluralistic grassroots movements.

(Escobar, 1995: 215)

The theory emphasises grassroots development and capacity building, given the inability of the state to curb deprivation and protect the common citizenry from structural violence and the scourge of capital machinations. Ziat (2007) notes that a number of criticisms have been levelled at the post-development school of thought, largely that their deductions are premised on facile binaries and exhibit methodological inconsistencies.

This short exposition reveals the complexities and contestations inherent in trying to define development; it reveals the importance of situatedness in defining development as well as the position power and hegemony occupy in shaping our understanding of development. If the major Western countries control dominant thinking around development based on a neo-liberal/neo-classical definition of development, then this will be infused into the global structures such as the IMF and World Bank, which can then promote their agenda of deregulation and the opening up of markets. This will inevitability have a huge impact on the conceptualisation and operationalisation of development paradigms. In equal measure, approaches to any other development school of thought will equally impact on attempts at development at the personal, local, national and global levels. Whist the intervention of youth and community development workers is often located within the personal and local strata of intervention, an appreciation of the structural layers allows us more effective intervention as it also locates itself in global structures of knowing and being.

Sustainable development/different dimensions of sustainable development

Moving on from the development discourse, it is significant to note that since the 1970s, sustainability has been injected into the development discourse to highlight not only economic growth but at the same time ensure the survival of the earth and its capital (human, social and natural). It could be argued that sustainable development was initially raised as an urgent issue premised on ecological concerns; however the increasing interconnectedness of the ecological, economic, cultural, political and technological has become more evidenced; hence the prevalent holistic approach to sustainable development.

The ecological question in sustainable development

Whilst the question of global inequality and its impact on communities and nations, and between nations, has been addressed in Chapter 3, it is important to highlight some of the concerns and counter views making up the ecological conundrum.

According to the Intergovernmental Panel on Climate Change (2008) in its publication *Climate Change 2007 Synthesis Report*, between 1995 and 2006, 11 out of the 12 years were ranked as the warmest in recorded history since 1850. There has been an average sea level rise since 1961 of 1.8mm, but from 1993 to 2007 the average was 3.1mm. There has been a palpable shrinking of the Arctic ice since 1978 at a rate of 2.7 per cent per decade and an increase in tropical cyclones since 1970 in North America. Furthermore, recent global warming can be linked to effects on terrestrial ecosystems that impact on animal and plant life. Some of this ecological degradation can be attributed to human activity, for example human-induced greenhouse gas emission has increased by 80 per cent between 1970 and 2004. These ecological concerns continue to cause the rise in sea levels, to affect wind and temperature patterns, and increase the extremities of hot days and cold nights, as well as the frequency of heat waves and droughts. Some of these concerns have led to urgent calls to save Mother Earth.

In relation to the ecological footprint, it is estimated that the average person uses 2.7 global hectares, however this varies from region to region with UAE and Qatar for example using 10 global hectares. It is estimated that in 2007, only 37 countries were responsible for two-thirds of the ecological footprint (Tormey, 2012). It is of further significance to note that the 31 OECD countries were responsible for 37 per cent of the earth's ecological footprint as opposed to only 12 per cent for the 10 ASEAN and 53 African countries combined (Tormey, 2012: 63). The conclusion is that we continue to exhaust the earth's resources faster than they can be replenished, and this raises urgent concerns about the continued existence of humanity; and more urgently, the question of what kind of earth our children and our children's children will inherit.

However it is important to note that a number of scientists doubt the veracity of the science behind sustainable development and dub it as suspect on the basis that climate change predictions are questionable; and that global warming is caused by natural processes and not necessarily by human design. This different school of thought posits that the cause of global warming is unknown and the causal links being made between global warming and human induced environmental destruction is not plausible (Syun-Ichi, 2007; Veizer, 2005; Tennekes, 2009).

Major conferences and developments

Whilst it can be said that notions of sustainable development were being raised as early as the 1960s (Elliot, 2013) it definitely gained palpable momentum in the early 1970s. In Stockholm 1972, a group of scientists commissioned by the

Club of Rome published *The Limits to Growth*, which highlighted concerns around accelerating industrialisation, rapid population growth, widespread malnutrition, depletion of non-renewable resources and a deteriorating environment (Meadows et al., 1972).

The urgency to address sustainable development was exacerbated in the mid-1980s by the discovery of a hole in the ozone layer in 1985 over Antarctica and the Chernobyl nuclear disaster in the same year. Whilst a huge site of contestation (Gibson, 2005) perhaps the best known definition of sustainable development is 'development that meets the needs of the present without compromising the ability of future generations to meet their own needs', articulated by the Brundtland Commission in its 1987 publication, *Our Common Future*. This was the report of the UN World Commission on Environment and Development, headed by former Norwegian Prime Minister Gro Harlem Brundtland. The UN set up a panel of 22 in 1984, sourced from both developed and developing countries, and this committee's report is contained in the *Our Common Future* (WCED 1987) report.

This report laid the pretext of the 1992 Rio de Janeiro Earth Summit which brought together 116 heads of state and over 8000 delegates. This summit is important in many ways, and it could be considered the most high profile environmental gathering up till then, bringing together such a diverse range of high profile actors, representative of both civil society organisations and governments. Of equal importance is the fact that it gave birth to Agenda 21, as well as other important covenants such as the Convention on Biodiversity and the Framework Convention on Climate Change (Elliot, 2013). According to Blewitt (2008: 18) the significance of Agenda 21 is that it offered:

> . . . *an action plan for sustainable development, integrating environmental with social and economic concerns, and articulating a participatory, community-based approach to a variety of issues, including population control, transparency, partnership working, equity and justice, and placing marketing principles within a regulatory framework.*

The UN Summit on Sustainable Development took place in Johannesburg, South Africa in 2002, and was more representative of divergent and unheard voices; it is also important to report the noteworthy recognition the conference accorded to the inextricability of sustainable development and the impact of globalisation on the poor.

The Rio+20 UN Summit focused on delivering the 'Green Economy' and future institutional framework for sustainable development. According to Elliot (2013: 11):

The notion of the green economy seeks an economic system that can address and prevent these crises whilst also protecting the earth's ecosystems, provide economic growth and contribute to poverty alleviation.

In relation to the institutional framework, it poses the question whether formal organisations, including the various arms of the UN 'are "fit for purpose" to guide, monitor, and coordinate progress towards sustainable development in the future'; with a particular focus on governance in relation to governments, private businesses and civil organisations in dealing with the question of sustainable development. The outcome document called for:

Renewal of political commitment; a call for development to be modelled on the Green economy in the context of sustainable development and poverty eradication; development of an Institutional framework for sustainable development; development of a Framework for action and follow-up; and developing a Means of implementation.

(UN Sustainable Development Knowledge Platform, online)

Whilst it should be acknowledged that the outcomes document has been one of the most comprehensive, it drew some criticism, including on the absence of some of the key actors like President Obama and Chancellor Merkel, as well as accusations of being watered down and shirking the tough decisions needed to arrest the Earth's unsustainable downward slide. Even the UN Secretary General Ban Ki-moon noted, 'Let me be frank. Our efforts have not lived up to the measure of the challenge' (UN Earth News, online).

Concept of sustainable development

Blewitt (2008) posits that four worldviews/perspectives can be identified in relation to conceptualisations of sustainable development.

- *Market liberals* argue that the growing environmental problems we face are caused by market failures and poor government policies in pursuit of economic growth.
- *Institutionalists* on the other hand argue that the present predicament can be predicated on the weak institutions and inadequate global cooperation, which has failed to correct environmental failures, promote development or counteract the self-interested nature of some states' actions.
- *Bio-environmentalists* blame the current sustainable impasse on unsustainable economic growth, overconsumption and unchecked materialism.
- *Social Greens* argue that 'large scale industrialisation and economic growth ... led to the acceleration of exploitation, inequality and

ecological injustice, leading to the erosion of local-community autonomy' (Blewitt, 2008: 4).

All of these four positions might give us perspectives on perceptions of sustainable development, however what they tend to converge on is the fact that there are many different dimensions of sustainable development beyond just the green and ecological facets.

In representations of sustainable development models (Elliot, 2013) the three main components of environment/ecology, society/social and economic/ market need to come together to represent a holistic picture of sustainable development. Arguably, focusing on one or two in the absence of the others often leads to unsustainable development. So the challenge then becomes, how do we all address all dimensions of development simultaneously and sustainably? However, diagrammatic representations of sustainable develop- ment are not all encompassing and exclusive; to the contrary, there might be many competing perspectives on offer. For example Elliot (2013) recognises more recent calls to incorporate a 'cultural diversity as the root of a more moral, spiritual, ethical and sustainable way of life' (p. 21).

The interrelationship between environmental, economic and social sustaina- bility has now come to be a mainstay in conceptualisations of sustainable development; there is an increasing recognition that to deal with one dimension of sustainability requires its relation to the other two, or more, dimensions; the symbiotic relationship between environmental and social sustainability is highlighted below:

*Many problems of resource depletion and environmental stress arise from disparities in economic and political power. An industry may get away with unacceptable levels of water pollution because the people who bear the brunt of it are poor and unable to complain effectively. A forest may be destroyed by excessive felling because the people living there have no alternatives or because timber contractors generally have more influence than forest dwellers. Globally, wealthier nations are better placed financially and technologically to cope with the effects of climatic change. **Hence, our inability to promote the common interest in sustainable development is often a product of the relative neglect of economic and social justice within and amongst nations.***

(World Commission on Environment and Development, 1987)

Elliot (2013: 15) posits that sustainable development can be 'seen to embrace concerns for environmental degradation, poverty and exclusion currently and regarding the long-term viability of existing approaches in both environment and development'. Blewitt (2008: 23) argues that sustainable development is multidimensional, encompassing social, ecological and economic goals and perspectives, and this breadth has led some critics to view the concept as vague, self-contradictory and incoherent, incapable of being put into practice; he calls it a 'dialogue of values' (Blewitt, 2008). However many writers have questioned the very foundations on which conceptualisations of sustainable development are built. Banerjee (2003) expresses the concern that concep-tualisations of sustainable development are often dominated by economic approaches to development rooted in colonialism. Cairns (2003) recognises that the whole arena of sustainable development is not an exact science but subject to negotiation, and in turn subjected to *situatedness*. These critical voices, mostly Southern perspectives, often put the concept under the microscope and question configurations of ways of knowing and being.

Sustainable development in a national context

The UK government has, in actively engaging with the major sustainable development initiatives since the early 1970s, developed principles of sustain-able development which emphasise the following:

1. Living within environmental limits.
2. Ensuring a strong, healthy and just society.
3. Achieving a sustainable economy.
4. Promoting good governance.
5. Using sound science responsibly.

(DEFRA 2005)

Whilst we explore development both at the personal and local levels, it is even more urgent to locate national and global contexts to our work. Whilst this chapter does not have the scope to explore sustainable development within the national context of the UK or any other given nation, we will strongly advise that readers of this book and practitioners try to locate their interventions within this given space.

Activity 1: Group Task

1. Conduct critical analyses of the selected Millennium Development Goals below and reflect on their advantages and disadvantages.
2. To what extent would meeting the Millennium Development Goals ensure sustainable development across the globe.
3. What are the causes of unsustainable development?

4. To what extend could youth and community workers/development workers work with communities at the personal, local, national and global levels to ensure sustainable development?
5. What theoretical approach to development do you subscribe to and how is it manifested in your praxis?

Selected Millennium Development Goals

Goal 1 Eradicate Extreme Poverty and Hunger
Target 1A: Halve, between 1990 and 2015, the proportion of people whose income is less than one dollar a day.
Target 1C: Halve, between 1990 and 2015, the proportion of people who suffer from hunger.

Goal 2 Achieve Universal Primary Education
Target 2A: Ensure that, by 2015, children everywhere, boys and girls alike, will be able to complete a full course of primary schooling.

Goal 3 Promote Gender Equality and Empower Women
Target 3A: Eliminate gender disparity in primary and secondary education, preferably by 2005, and to all levels of education no later than 2015.

Goal 4 Reduce Child Mortality
Target 4A: Reduce by two thirds, between 1990 and 2015, the under-five mortality rate.

Goal 5 Improve Maternal Health
Target 5A: Reduce by three quarters, between 1990 and 2015, the maternal mortality ratio.

Goal 6 Combat HIV/AIDS, Malaria and Other Diseases
Target 6A: Have halted by 2015 and begun to reverse the spread of HIV/AIDS.
Target 6C: Have halted by 2015 and begun to reverse the incidence of malaria and other major diseases.

Goal 7 Ensure Environmental Sustainability
Target 7A: Integrate the principles of sustainable development into country policies and programmes and reverse the loss of environmental resources.
Target 7C: Halve by 2015 the proportion of people without sustainable access to safe drinking water and basic sanitation.
Target 7D: By 2020 to have achieved a significant improvement in the lives of at least 100 million slum dwellers.

Conclusion

We started by exploring the elusive concept of development as well as the many theoretical perspectives on development. We then explored: the notion of sustainable development and the major milestones/highlights since the 1970s; raising the ecological question along the way; and very deliberately refraining from postulating our position. We also noted that the many dimensions of sustainable development are inextricably linked to each other; and this symbiosis requires a holistic approach. This is important as we are keen on encouraging the reader to explore a range of perspectives before making up their mind.

Overall, this chapter has been concerned with exploring a range of perspectives on development as well as critically analysing its very epistemological and phenemological base. It is easily deductable, from the overview, to see that the concept of development is multifaceted and shrouded in contestations; and to a large extent is influenced by hegemonic and dominant *situatedness*. As practitioners mainly operating at the personal and local levels, we need to understand structures and how the globalisation of development impacts on our praxis; and then how we can work with communities to support them take action, to reverse underdevelopment trends. Global Youth Work is this area of work, focusing on how young people are engaged. It is the subject of our next chapter.

Reference

Amin, S. (2006) The Millennium Development Goals: A Critique from the South. *Monthly Review Press*, 57: 10, available at www.monthlyreview.org/0306amin.htm

Banerjee, S.B. (2003) Who Sustains Whose Development? Sustainable Development and the Reinvention of Nature. *Organization Studies*, 24(1), 143–180.

Blewitt, J. (2008) *Understanding Sustainable Development*. London: Earthscan.

Cairns, J. (2003) Integrating Top-down/Bottom-up Sustainability Strategies: an Ethical Challenge. *Ethics in Science and Environmental Politics*, 2003: 1–6

Daly, T. and Regan, C. (2012) Development: The Story of an Idea. In Regan, C. (Ed.) *Development in an Unequal World*. South Africa: UNISA Press.

Department for Environment, Food and Rural Affairs (2005) *Securing the Future: Delivering the UK Government Sustainable Development Strategy*. London: DEFRA.

Elliot, J. (2013) *An Introduction to Sustainable Development*. 4th Edition. New York: Routledge.

Escobar, A. (1992) Imagining a Post-Development Era? Critical Thought, Development and Social Movements. *Social Text*. 31: 32, 20–56.

Escobar, A. (1995) *Encountering Development: The Making and Unmaking of the Third World*. New Jersey: Princeton University Press.

Escobar, A. (2000) Beyond the Search for a Paradigm: Post-Development and Beyond. *Development (SID)*, 43: 4, 11–4.

Gibson, R.B. (2005) *Sustainability Assessment*. London: Earthscan.

Haq, M. ul (1995) *Reflections on Human Development*. Oxford: Oxford University Press.

Intergovernmental Panel on Climate Change (2008) *Climate Change 2007 Synthesis Report*. Geneva: IPCC.

Kay, C. and Gwynne, R. (2000) Relevance of Structuralist and Dependency Theories in the Neoliberal Period: A Latin American Perspective. In Harris, R. and Seid, M.J. *Critical Perspectives on Globalisation Neoliberalsim in the Developing Countries*. London: Brill.

Meadows, D.H., Meadows, D.L., Randers, J. and Behrens, W.W. (1972) *The Limits to Growth: A Report to The Club of Rome*. New York: Universe Books.

Nussbaum, M. (2000) *Women and Human Development: The Capabilities Approach*. Cambridge: Cambridge University Press.

Pieterse, J. N. (2009) *Development Theory*. 2nd edition. London: Sage.

PlanYourPlace (online) *What is a Sustainable City?* accessed Sept. 2013 at: http://planyourplace.ca/pypblog/?p=44

Rahnema, M. (1997) Towards Post-Development: Searching for Signposts, A New Language and New Paradigms. In Rahnema, M. with Bawtree, V. (Eds.) *The Post Development Reader*. New York: Zed Books.

Rostow, W. (1960) *The Stages of Economic Growth: A Non-Communist Manifesto*. Cambridge University Press: Cambridge.

Sen, A. (1993) Capability and Well-being. In Martha Nussbaum, C. and Sen, A. (Eds.) *The Quality of Life*. Oxford: Clarendon Press.

Sen, A. (1995) *Inequality Reexamined*. Cambridge: Harvard University Press.

Sen, A. (1999a) *Commodities and Capabilities*. New York: Oxford University Press.

Sen, A. (1999b) *Development and Freedom*. Oxford: Oxford University Press.

Sen, A. (2005) Human Rights and Capabilities. *Journal of Human Development and Capabilities*, 6: 2 151–66.

Stanton, E. (2007) *The Human Development Index: A History*. Working Paper Series, Number 127. MA: University of Massachusetts-Amherst.

Syun-Ichi, A, (2007). *On the Fundamental Defect in the IPCC's Approach to Global Warming Research. Climate Science: Roger Pielke Sr*. wordpress.com. Retrieved 31 August 2012.

Tennekes, H. (2009) *A Skeptical View of Climate Models*. www.sepp.org/NewSEPP/Climate%20models-Tennekes.htm

Thomas, A. (2000) Poverty and the End of Development. In Allen, T. and Thomas, A. (Eds.) *Poverty and Development into the 21st Century*. Oxford: Oxford University Press/Open University.

Tormey, R. (2012) Sustainability: The Defining Development Issue. In Regan, C. (Ed.) *Development in an Unequal World*. South Africa: UNISA Press.

UN Earth News (online) *Rio+20: A Lesson in Communication*. http://unearthnews.org/rio20-a-lesson-in-communications-3/

UN Sustainable Development Knowledge Platform (online) *Future We Want – Outcome Document*. http://sustainabledevelopment.un.org/futurewewant.html

UNDP (2010) *Human Development Report 2010: The Real Wealth of Nations:* Pathways to Human Development. New York: UNDP.

Veizer, J. (2005) Celestial Climate Driver: A Perspective from Four Billion Years of the Carbon Cycle. *Geoscience Canada*. 1: 32 (Retrieved 26 August 2012).

World Commision on Environment and Development (1987) *Our Common Future*. Oxford: Oxford University Press.

Ziat, A. (2007) *Exploring Post-development* Theory and Practice, Problems and Perspectives. New York: Routledge.

CHAPTER 5

What is Global Youth Work?

Introduction

In this book's developing narrative so far, we have explored the concept and process of globalisation, establishing that time, space and distance have been conquered; we have also shown that this has led to the intensification of consciousness with economic, political, cultural, environmental and technological vibrations. We have further established that the very construction and interpretation of social reality is affected by our *situatedness* in relation to the globalisation project. Whether globalisation benefits us or destroys our livelihoods is then a tale of two cities. We have gone on to look at the grotesque nature of inequality including the health, education and economic dimensions, concluding that structural violence is wrought on a huge part of the Earth's population disproportionately and against the very principles of social justice. We have looked at development and sustainable development in attempting to lift people out of poverty, deprivation and human suffering; we have looked at various models of development as well as the major initiatives to engender sustainable development, especially at the structural and global levels.

Consequently, this chapter will continue the narrative and explore how action can be taken by individuals and communities to change the way things are. It will start by locating the pedagogical tool of Global Youth Work within the wider development field; it will attempt to clarify the terminology used in the field of Global Youth Work as opposed to in its conceptual location. We will then review various definitions of Global Youth Work and the existing conceptual models; we will attempt to theorise the field of Global Youth Work, which continues to exhibit a lacunae of theoretical deficit. In conclusion, this chapter will propose key competences and principles in attempting to offer a theoretical basis of Global Youth Work. It will argue that the central role of Global Youth Work is to provoke consciousness and support young people to take action that is commensurate to their activities, whatever they deem it to be.

Objectives

1. To explore definitions and theoretical perspectives of Global Youth Work.
2. To identify key principles and competences in the field of Global Youth Work.

3. To explore counter-orthodoxy and critical Southern perspectives in the field of Global Youth Work.
4. To demonstrate that the practice of Global Youth Work is underpinned by social justice and anti-oppressive practice.
5. To understand how provoking consciousness and taking action constitute the twin cardinal constituencies of the Global Youth Work arena.

Global Youth Work

Globalisation, as a process, continues to affect all human beings in a number of ways including in communications, technology, ecology, economics, work organisation, culture and civil society (Beck, 2000). In a similar vein, Sallah (2008b) identified the five faces of globalisation as economical, technological, cultural, environmental and political. All of these faces are visited on young people without choice and these considerations, practised informally and based on the principles of youth work, is what Global Youth Work is about. It can be argued that the concept of Global Youth Work has existed in many guises previously, including International Youth Work and Development Education. However, the term GYW was coined in 1995 (Bourn and McCollum, 1995) and its prominence has grown in recent times as a distinct way of working with young people, incorporating both the principles of Development Education and youth work. It is worth noting that in the UK, there appear to be efforts to decapitate youth work in the mainstream through government policy (DMU, 2013) and Global Youth Work, whilst still widely practiced, must be understood in this context. Perhaps the best known definition of Global Youth Work is that of the Development Education Association (now Think Global):

Informal education with young people that encourages a critical understanding of the links between the personal, local and the global and seeks their active participation in actions that bring about change towards greater equality and justice.

(DEA, 2004: 21)

It is an educational approach that 'opens people's eyes and minds to the realities of the globalised world and awakens them to bring about a world of greater justice, equity and Human Rights for all' (North-South Centre, 2010: 10). It is a methodological approach that explores the personal, local, national and global interconnections between young people and the five faces of globalisation, interactively to generate a critical understanding (Freire, 1972) which hopefully leads to the second prerogative of promoting action as a result of that consciousness which attempts to change the world (Sallah, 2008a: 7).

Terminology and conceptualisation

Whilst in the field of youth work, this concept is largely known as Global Youth Work (Sallah, 2009a; Cotton, 2009), related ideas have gone by many other names, such as Global Learning, or Education for Sustainable Development and Global Citizenship (ESDGC). *Dare to Stretch* (2009) states that this aspect of working with young people to address the global dimension is called: 'Global Youth Work' in Northern Ireland, England and Scotland; 'Development Education in Youth Work' and 'Global Justice in Youth Work' in Ireland; and 'Education for Sustainable Development and Global Citizenship' in Wales. As already argued (Sallah, 2009a, 2008c), Development Education is the umbrella term used in the field and according to Bourn (2008: 1) this term 'first emerged during the 1970s, in part in response to the growth of development and aid organisations and the decolonisation process' as well as through the influence of UNESCO and the United Nations (Bourn, 2008).

As demonstrated in my research (Sallah, 2008c, 2009a) the terminology used to define the work is inextricably linked to its conceptualisation. It is cardinal that we distinguish between terminology and conceptualisation from the outset. Terminology is used here to refer to the descriptive label which is used to describe the domain in question. Conceptualisation conversely denotes how it is *understood*; in other words to what ranges of activities, processes and topics the domain refers. Conceptualisation refers furthermore to how this is understood, processed and integrated into teaching and professional practice by the individuals, and also by the institutions, that are involved. Terminology and conceptualisation are not the same (and should not be viewed as such) but despite this they are inextricably linked together and as such need to be analysed and evaluated alongside one another.

I conducted research in 2008 to explore the state of Global Youth Work in British Higher Education Institutions (Sallah 2008c, 2009a). Three complementary strategies were used in order to improve the validity of the research through triangulation: 43 individual interviews were conducted with either course or module leaders out of a possible 50 across the UK; the second element to the overall approach was a focus group comprised of 11 individuals from some of the leading organisations in the statutory service, International Non-governmental Organisations and HEIs involved in Development Education/ Global Youth Work; the third approach was semi-structured telephone interviews with 28 recent graduates of JNC or equivalent qualifying courses. This was a dimensional sample taking into consideration course level, geographical location as well as gender. It is based on this research that I make the following observations in relation to the conceptualisation and terminology of Global Youth Work.

In relation to terminology, nine of the HEI interviewees called it what can broadly be described under the umbrella term of 'global youth work' (these responses included the terms 'international youth work' and 'local and global perspectives in youth and community development'). These responses can be interpreted as having clear links and objectives related to work with young people and/or communities. There is a clear correlation in this terminology between the theoretical concepts of 'global' work with young people and the *practice* of work with young people.

Four of the interviewees called it global education and awareness. Whilst it may be assumed that due to the use of the word 'education' there is a level of relationship between the knowledge of global issues and work with communities and young people, this may not be the case. The 'global education' aspect may in fact relate to the academic, personal and professional development of the students participating in these programmes, rather than the practical skills and knowledge of how to embed and implement this knowledge in practice.

Five participants used terms related to the process and concept of globalisation (including 'global and international', 'managing change in a global context', 'globalisation' and 'youth in a changing society'). This suggests a level of understanding of both the process and concept of globalisation and global issues on the part of the lecturer delivering these modules but, with the exception of the module making direct reference to 'youth', there is no immediate signifier to practice links for students.

Four responses referred to what could be deemed 'global citizenship'. Again, this terminology suggests development of personal skills and knowledge with no direct reference to the practical skills and knowledge required by a youth and community practitioner.

Nine respondents did not identify development education/Global Youth Work in any way, whilst a further six interviewees named it as one of a number of different things that could not be classified into any of the previous headings. Some of these included 'mission shaped practice' (clearly identifying faith as a driver for the learning), 'cross cultural studies' (which may or may not make direct links to global work with young people or globalisation – it could relate solely to practice within local communities), 'counter hegemonic approach' and Education for Sustainable Development and Global Citizenship (ESDGC; see Welsh Assembly Government, 2008).

There is a level of synergy indentified across some of the responses by HEI participants, predominantly within the first group identified, where nine of the responses included, in some way, the terms 'youth/community work' and 'global'. This suggests it is underpinned by a clear understanding of youth and community work within a global context, firmly contextualised within youth work processes. This therefore makes it very different from other terms classified which do not clearly identify or make the links with the processes involved with youth work and informal education. The conceptualisation of development education/Global Youth Work also differs from organisation to organisation, not only between HEIs. Six terms were identified that related to development education/Global Youth Work that was utilised by the organisations involved in the research.

From the above analyses and based on my experience of interacting with the Development Education field, the term Active Global Citizenship is largely used within the field of formal teacher training, and the term Development Education is largely used within the international non-government/charity organisations, but even within this arena there are differences. Some organisations, such as the British Red Cross, use the term Humanitarian Education, whilst the common term used in Wales is Education for Sustainable Development and Global Citizenship (ESDGC): the former addresses the International Humanitarian Law and education agenda, whilst the latter focuses on the combined agenda of global citizenship and sustainable development education.

I delivered two staff training days separately for Oxfam and Y Care in 2010, to support them to critically reflect on the work they carry out with young people around global issues. It is interesting to note that Oxfam labelled its work 'Campaign Work' which focused on a preset agenda and fundraising; and Y Care called its work around these issues outside the UK 'Youth Focused International Development', although it delivers one of the most comprehensive packages of Global Youth Work in the UK. Whilst some of these terminologies and conceptualisations might be similar to Global Youth Work, the divergence exists because Global Youth Work is based on youth work principles which centre on an informal approach based on experiential learning, mostly revolving around the voluntary engagement of young people as well as 'tipping the balance of power in young people's favour' (Young, 2006; Davies, 2005) in contrast to the Development Education approach which sometimes has an explicit campaign agenda linked to it, for example raising funds, as in the case of Oxfam highlighted earlier. Global Youth Work therefore, whilst retaining most of Development Education's principles, is in addition grounded in youth work principles, with the basis of starting from the young people's agenda and experiences. The Development Education Association articulates this difference very well in the following quotation:

> *Global youth work is a form of development education. However, what makes global youth work distinct is that it **starts from young people's own perspectives and experiences and develops a negotiated agenda for learning**. Global youth work also focuses primarily on the impact of globalisation in the UK and overseas rather than education about the **development and underdevelopment** of countries. Although it shares many of the values and principles that underpin good youth work, development education often has its own agenda from the outset, linked to specific campaigns or concerns and has historically taken place in more formal educational settings.*

(DEA, 2004: 28; original emphasis)

Global Youth Work conceptual frameworks

Figures 5.1, 5.2 and 5.3 posit Global Youth Work conceptual frameworks, and we can observe some synergies and divergences in the conceptualisations of Global Youth Work. In Figure 5.1, the North-South Centre postulates that Global Education enables the development of skills, knowledge and attitudes needed for everyone to fulfil their potential and live in a just and sustainable

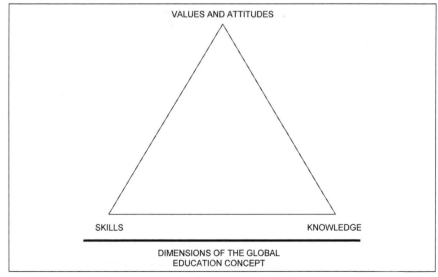

Figure 5.1   Reproduced from North-South Centre, 2010

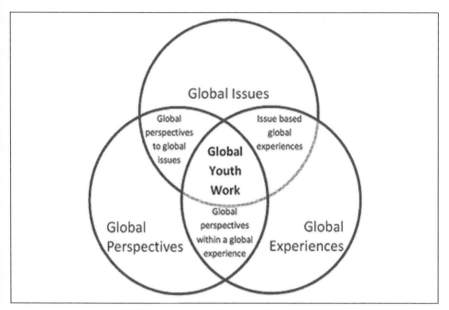

Figure 5.2 Reproduced from Woolley, 2011

Figure 5.3 Reproduced from Williams, S. and Edleston, J. (Eds), 2010

world (North-South Centre, 2010: 16). This concept proposes the reimagining of the content, form and context of education, with a focus on developing the necessary skills, knowledge, values and attitudes.

In the second diagram, Woolley (2011) presents the three dimensions of global issues, global experiences and global perspectives that must be configured as a whole for the distinct practice of Global Youth Work to emerge; he argues that only a single dimension being addressed, in the absence of the others, leaves it short of Global Youth Work. The global issue in the overlapping circles focuses on the interconnectedness of the personal and local issues, linked to the global. In his diagrammatic representation, Woolley (2011) argues that young people need to be exposed to a global experience to understand the interconnectedness, however this global experience does not necessarily mean leaving national boundaries, and leaving national boundaries does not also necessarily guarantee a global experience; he argues that Global Youth Work must create that global experience, regardless of spatial location. The third dimension of global perspective, he argues, is the often missing majority or Southern perspective in Global Youth Work; this perspective of seeing the world, from Southern and counter-orthodoxy perspectives, is a cardinal and essential part of the configured whole of Global Youth Work.

In the third diagram, Williams and Edleston (2010) advance that the first function of Global Youth Work is to support young people to connect with local-global issues, and to encourage them to challenge their own construction of reality and the normalisation of inequality and injustice, starting from their own realities and experiences; and then to bring about change. This model has been found particularly useful and simple to understand by young people and practitioners (Cotton, 2009).

Re-theorising Global Youth Work

In attempting to re-theorise Global Youth Work, it is pivotal that I clarify two issues: the first is the distinct practice of youth work which is the foundation of Global Youth Work as a pedagogical tool; the second is the influence of Paulo Freire in my thinking and the articulation of my conceptual model.

The distinct practice of youth work

How do practitioners grapple with global issues; not only in all aspects of work with young people, but more especially in the distinct practice of youth work? Youth work can be postulated as a distinct way of working with young people where youth workers are 'seeing and responding to them simply as young people, as untouched as possible by pre . . . set labels' (Davies, 2005: 18). Whilst there are many spaces in which work with young people takes place, for example when teachers encounter young people as students or when Youth Offending practitioners engage young people as young offenders, the process of youth work is different from these encounters. First, encounters between youth workers and young people remain largely voluntary, take part in informal spaces and start from young people's territories literally and metaphorically (Young, 2006; Davies, 2005). Second, the agenda for youth work, whilst sometimes negotiated, is largely determined by young people themselves and based on their every day realities, rooted in locality, their networks and experiential learning (Kolb, 1984; Jeffs and Smith, 2002; Davies, 2005, 2010). Consequently, youth work is about supporting young people to deconstruct their taken-for-granted reality, the way in which they have previously viewed and interacted with the world. Youth work then seeks to support them to develop new ways of looking and interacting with the world, especially in instances where established realities have either been oppressive to the young people concerned, or where the young people may themselves be unwitting beneficiaries of the oppressive structures of society. This distinct method of working with young people:

> . . . *provides space for association, activity, dialogue and action. And it provides support, opportunity and experience for young people as they move from childhood to adulthood. In today's Europe, it is guided and governed by principles of participation and empowerment, values of human rights and democracy, and anti-discrimination and tolerance.*
>
> (Declaration of the 1st European Youth Work Convention, 2010: 2)

It is necessary to be transparent at this point that there are many who do not subscribe to the 'purist' notion of youth work. Wylie (2010) highlights the various responses to what he describes as 'youth work in a cold climate': the romantics, he argues are those who hang on to the notions of good old fashioned youth work; the technocrats are those who hinge their practice on managerialism and the dictates of targets and accreditation with scant regard for youth work processes; whilst the principled pragmatists, and Wylie considers himself one, believe that the process of youth work must evolve to survive in a presently cold climate of government cuts and in some cases complete annihilation of whole youth services. These three different positions aptly capture the debate raging in the youth work field in relation to the future direction of travel for youth work. These different positions also highlight the complexities involved in presenting the distinct practice of youth work in a dynamic environment. However despite the varied positions, most social commentators (Wylie, 2010; Davies, 2010) agree on the fundamental principles of youth work: mainly experiential and informal learning premised on a negotiated agenda with young people. Youth work, therefore, is more than just education about the workings of oppression. The traditional didactic relationship between teacher and pupil can itself be seen as both an outcome and a sustainer of particular constructed ideas of difference. If youth work is not to mirror such processes, the education it proposes must be a very different type of process, underpinned by very different types of values. The ideas for this process and for these values are contained in the work of Paulo Freire.

The influence of Freire

Freire (1972, 1974, 1985, 1995) has influenced my work through his advocacy of education for liberation and his belief in the transformative power of education to bring about social change. The most fascinating aspect of my encounter with Freire's work has been his ability to identify the key processes that, subsequent to his work, have come to inform what it is we do as community educators and youth work practitioners. His assertion is that all education is political, implicitly or explicitly, as well as that education can serve to liberate or domesticate. Domestification, he argues, is rooted in the banking concept of education where the student is the bank and the teacher deposits knowledge during lessons and retrieves the knowledge during exams. Freire sees this as a dysfunctional approach that serves only to reproduce and replicate the very structures that oppress, as the education is then not rooted in the reality of the oppressed. In contrast, Freire advocates for education rooted in the pedagogy of liberation; a transformative education that is rooted in the reality of the students which is geared towards enabling the students to gain critical consciousness in order to name and transform their world. Although some have argued (Smith, 2002; Taylor, 1993) that Freire's approach to education, whilst radical, was often positioned as either/or (black or white), ignoring the many possibilities in between and that the educational encounters he explores remain largely formal. Regardless of this criticism, his incisive perception of the power of transformative education remains illuminative and resonates with my practice and values. It has greatly influenced my thinking, and my approach in both teaching and practice has been to use transformative education to attempt to get youth workers to deconstruct their reality and effectively change their practice as a means of bringing about social change in the particular areas this book seeks to address. My approach to working with constructed notions of globalisation and global inequality has been to work with practitioners to, first deconstruct their reality by rooting their intervention in their learning, and then to work with them to transform their practice on their new found reality. The work of Freire is based on the notion that the message of education is as much in the process of how education is conducted as in the content, and his work centres on equalizing the relationship between educators and their communities so that education becomes a mutual process which he calls dialogical: education with people, not education of people. It follows that those exploring the best ways to conduct informal education with oppressed groups need to pay attention to working with, not working on, communities.

A critical look at existing models: towards a new paradigm

From the preceding discourse on conceptual models, we can deduct that whilst some conceptual frameworks focus on the development of skills and attitudes (for example North-South Centre) and others focus on connecting with the young people as key (for example Williams and Edleston, 2010) all three of the concepts focus on process, based not on a fixed curriculum, but on the constructed realities of the young people engaged and on the need to develop critical literacy and to support action that young people choose, to change the world. The commonality of all these three models is that the process of engagement starts from where young people are at and develops from the personal to the global. All three models are extremely helpful ways of theorising Global Youth Work, however, with the exception of Woolley (2011) to a limited extent, the models advanced do not necessarily infuse a critical Southern perspective. This often leaves Global Youth Work to operate from the 'Missionary position' (Sallah, 2008) where the whole objective of the intervention is to 'Christianise and civilise', following in the colonial trail of the oppressive genesis of development education, with its roots in colonial subjugation. This kind of missionary approach has the potential to replicate oppression and breed notions of charity instead of interdependence; it also has the tendency to operate from a position of negative neutrality where the configurations of normality we premise our actions are on a defective logic, in Freirian parlance. Joseph et al. (2002) call for an inclusive Black perspective that should move away from the margins into the centrality of mainstream thinking and action; they define a Black perspective in Global Youth Work as:

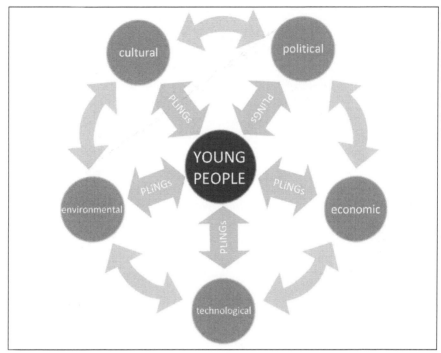

Figure 5.4   Five faces and PLiNGs

A perspective that aims to strive for global democracy and place Black people at the forefront of global and local decision-making. Far from being kept on the fringes of global society, Black people ought to be at the heart of global society, securing fair and just rewards for their contributions to a shared and interdependent world. The majority world cannot simply be ignored or wished away.

I have consistently argued (Sallah, 2008b, 2009a, 2013a, 2013b) that Global Youth Work must first attempt to engage with young people's constructed reality and then support young people to make the links between the personal, local, national and global, and the five dimensions of globalisation (economic, political, cultural, technological and environmental) to provoke critical consciousness; and then support them to take action, whatever the concerned young people deem appropriate in creating a more just world for themselves and the rest of humanity. My conceptual model (Figure 5.4) of Global Youth Work (Sallah, 2011a) places young people at the centre and in constant interaction with the five faces and at the Personal, Local, National and Global (PLiNG) to the extent that any issue can be located within this matrix. This model is not

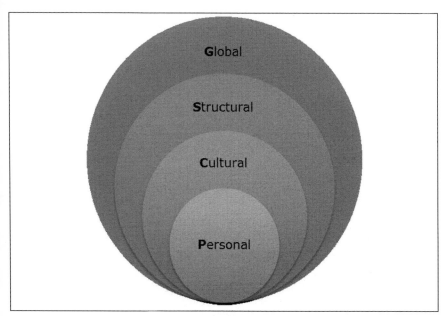

Figure 5.5   PCSG Model

Eurocentric and subsumed in Northern hegemonic notions of domination and construction of reality. It has been influenced by Althusser's (1971) Repressive State Apparatus and Ideological State Apparatuses, and by Thompson's (2003) PCS (Personal, Cultural, Structural) model of oppression, but with another layer added to it as depicted in Figure 5.5. Oppression and discrimination must be understood not only at the personal, local, national and global but also with an interactive global dimension that is symbiotic to all the other layers.

Freire's concept (1972) of critical consciousness has greatly influenced my thinking around Global Youth Work praxis as stated earlier. Figures 5.6 and 5.7 illustrate my thinking and how Freire influences it. In Figure 5.6, I present the role of the practitioner/youth worker in either intervening or engaging with the young person or collective to deconstruct and reconstruct their reality as a site of struggle. This is linked to Freire's premise that oppression is based on a false consciousness; in this case a false consciousness of how inequality and neoliberal orthodoxy are normalised. In the second diagram, I explain how a dialogical and mutual process of engagement, that negates the banking concept of education, where the youth worker acts as an external catalyst to the oppressed reality of the young people,

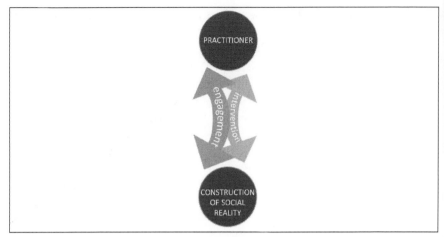

Figure 5.6   GYW in practice

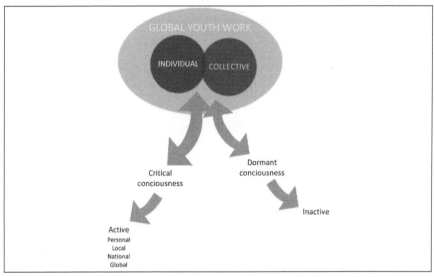

Figure 5.7   Provoking consciousness

is involved in provoking consciousness. This consciousness can either be critical, what Freire calls critical transivity or what I call dormant consciousness, where the young person gets the information or knowledge but is not yet able to locate it in their reality, possibly due to what Freire (1972) calls 'fear of freedom'; or the different pieces of the jigsaw not yet coming together. Freire's contribution to my thinking is essential, as I have gone on to adapt and apply his thinking in my work.

In the same vein, my philosophy to learning is influenced by the Participatory Action Research (Chambers, 1983; Jayakaran, 1996; Baum et al., 2006; Chambers, 2007) approach to generating knowledge, which sees the researcher and the researched as both contributors of knowledge. By the same logic, my praxis recognises the existing knowledge that young people have, and it seeks to engage them in a liberatory and dialogical approach to education where both learner and student are mutual producers and consumers of knowledge; as well as utilising methodological approaches of engagement that start from where they are, on the basis of voluntary engagement in line with the distinct approach of youth work discussed earlier. Whilst the power imbalance that exists between the practitioner and young people is recognised, an important part of the Global Youth Work intervention/engagement is working to equalise this power imbalance, supporting young people to gain critical literacy and being more informed in taking ownership of their actions. It is not about indoctrination, but significantly about young people going through processes to liberate themselves. As the late Burkina Faso president stated, consciousness cannot be granted, it must be conquered (Sankara, 1987). Without young people gaining that critical consciousness and taking ownership of the resulting action, then the intervention cannot be sustainable: it is my experience that the gains will dissipate as soon as those who parachute in and impose on their lives are gone. Sometimes young people choose to do something that the practitioner vehemently disagrees with, to the extent that the practitioner regrets their initial engagement with the young people. And that is ok, for the way of the Global Youth Work path is to provoke consciousness, not to enforce a version of constructed reality. Youth work practitioners need to equalise the power imbalance and negotiate with young people.

The intersecting and multiple identities that are constructed for young people, as well as the ones they construct for themselves, have been significant, especially in exploring variables like religion, class, gender, ethnicity and geographical location; for example to understand the constructed identities of young Muslims requires us to understand the global impact of the Muslim Ummah, their constructed identities, perhaps as Black British or Asian British for example, as well as in which part of the world they are located and how neo-liberal projections of globalisation impact on them. These constructed realities are the domains of Global Youth Work and deciphering the multiple and fluid identities in an age of globality are of great urgency.

The place of social justice in the pedagogy of Global Youth Work is often suspect, frequently occupying an afterthought position, rather than occupying a central position in the dispensation of the praxis. Where conceptualisations of Global Youth Work are based on notions of Northern hegemony over the South as a given; where the success of the North is premised on the misery of the South; where the relationship is based on exploitation and oppression manifested in structural violence brought to bear from those afar: our priorities and notions of justice might not seem so urgent. But having engaged in Global Youth Work both in the South and in the North, I see there is a need for Global Youth Work to be involved in the fierce urgency of imbuing social justice as a cardinal plank of Global Youth Work.

In advancing a new thesis of Global Youth Work, it is important to highlight again that Global Youth Work:

(a) Is concerned with how the concept and process of globalisation impacts on young people's realities

As there is increasing interconnectedness and intensification of how the process of globalisation impacts on Mother Earth and its inhabitants economically, environmentally, culturally, politically and technologically, as demonstrated in Chapter 1, Global Youth Work must be concerned with making the personal, local, national and global links between young people's existence and how these dimensions affect their lives. From the food they eat, the clothes they wear, the air they breathe, the gadgets they use – ranging from a laptop to an iPhone – to the political systems that determine their existence; young people must be supported to understand their existence within the complex matrix of interconnectedness. Global Youth Work is not just about working with young people, but fundamentally addressing their correlation to the local, national and global.

(b) Is based on the principles of informal education and youth work

Global Youth Work, like youth work, is a different way of working with young people; it is premised on a number of planks, including: equalising the power imbalance between young people and practitioner; mostly voluntary engagement of young people; informal approaches to working with young people; and a focus on developing critical literacy. It is an approach where there is a negotiation with young people and the constant remains the empowerment of young people.

(c) Is located in young people's realities

Global Youth Work seeks to address what might at times appear to be complex interconnections between the personal, local, national and global in constant interaction with the five faces (see Figure 5.4); and ultimately to change the world. For this reason, it is extremely important that the intervention/ engagement starts from young people's daily realities, in line with informal approaches to education. Informal education is rooted in experiential learning (Kolb, 1984; Jeffs and Smith, 2002) as well as in young people's networks; and therefore, in line with earlier conceptual models discussed, it must start from where young people are at. It must start and be located in young people's daily realities and eventually stretch young people to new territories and new opportunities.

(d) Challenges oppression and promotes social justice

The central plank of Global Youth Work, in my opinion, is to challenge oppression and promote social justice. This is fundamentally premised on the fact that, as demonstrated in earlier chapters, there is grotesque inequality, structural violence and abject poverty based on the greed of some, in a world where 80% of the world's resources are consumed by 20% of the world's population. This surely cannot be right, even if we have been seduced by the defective logic of the system, as Freire would put it. Global Youth Work must be brave in debunking the positions of negative neutrality and explicitly postulating a social justice position. Whilst every fundamentalist position is supported by their version of the 'truth', we cannot use that as an excuse to adopt a lackadaisical position of principle towards social justice. My position on Global Youth Work, based on my experiences and research, is motivated by my desire to challenge oppression and promote social justice. I am very transparent about my position and I am very open to democratic challenge; I challenge practitioners to set up their positions and be transparent, but at the same time be open to democratic challenge.

(e) Promotes consciousness and action

Global Youth Work should be, in my experience, a pedagogical mechanism to provoke consciousness and support young people to take action. People in general, and young people as a focus of our discussion, have come to accept reality as a given because that is the way things are. They might be oblivious to their hegemonic dependence on others, and to the fact that their advantage is premised on the disadvantage of those others who, as an extreme example, perceive their disadvantage as a divine act beyond question and wallow in a state of hopelessness. Global Youth Work must engage young people to first gain critical consciousness, in order to be able to question given realities. This is important for two reasons: for those who benefit from the status quo to understand the true basis of their advantage; and for those who consume the dregs of society and lose themselves in a catatonic state of helplessness and hopelessness to understand the true nature of their oppression. Principally, this process, by way of informal education approaches, must seek to provoke young people's consciousness. It is not about analysing and giving young people a to-do list but rather a dialogical approach where both practitioner and young people are teachers and learners, actors and doers symbiotically and simultaneously. It is one with the object of synthesising young people's existence with their lived realities.

The second component of this project, then, is in line with Amartha Sen's capabilities and capacitation approaches to development. Supporting young people to gain the skills, knowledge and values they need to translate their newfound consciousness into reality. As stated earlier, it might not be the action we judge to be the best but it is the action that young people, after gaining critical consciousness, have judged to be the best. The practitioner must constantly and continuously engage young people in democratic dialogues and support them to continuously analyse and reflect on their actions.

Conclusion

We have explored various definitions of Global Youth Work, establishing that it is not a universal given; additionally the terminology used and the corresponding conceptualisations do not always necessarily correlate. However we have identified the terminology of Global Youth Work, on the basis of merging the practice of Youth Work and Development Education. We have reviewed a range of conceptual models and concluded by advancing the five faces and PLiNG model in reconceptualising Global Youth Work with a particular focus on: the impact of globalisation on young people; the principles of informal education and Global Youth Work; locating it in young people's realities; challenging oppression and promoting social justice; and basing it on provoking consciousness and supporting action.

This approach to working with young people to critically explore local-global issues and support young people to take the action they choose to take, is one of many responses to global inequality, exploitation, deprivation, oppressions and a state of hopelessness. A range of responses, from ethical consumerism to the frequent demonstrations against the Bretton Woods Institutions to fair-trade initiatives, are attempts to build a more equitable world. Based on this quest for social justice, those who advocate for and practice Global Youth Work must transparently and unashamedly declare this mantra.

References

Althusser, L. (1971) Ideology and Ideological State Apparatuses. In Althusser, L. (Ed.) *Lenin and Philosophy and other Essays*. New York: Monthly Review Press.

Baum, F., MacDougall, C. and Smith, D. (2006) Participatory Action Research. *Journal of Epidemiol Community Health*, 60: 854–7.

Beck, U. (2000) *What is Globalisation?* Cambridge: Polity Press.

Bourn, D. (2008) *Development Education, Debates and Dialogues*. London: Institute of Education.

Bourn, D. and McCollum, A. (Eds.) (1995) *A World of Difference: Making Global Connections in Youth Work*. London: Development Education Association.

Chambers, R. (1983). *Rural Development: Putting The Last First*. London: Longman.

Chambers, R. (2007) *From PRA to PLA and Pluralism: Practice and Theory*. IDS Working Paper 286. Brighton: Institute of Development Studies.

Cotton, N. (2009) *Global Youth Work in the UK: Research Report*. London: DEA.

Dare to Stretch (2009) *Promoting Development Education in Youth Work Training, A Research Report on Development Education in Community Youth Work Courses at the University of Ulster, Jordanstown*. Belfast: Centre for Global Education.

Davies, B. (2005) Youth Work: A Manifesto For Our Times. *Youth and Policy*, 88: 1–23.

Davies, B. (2010) Straws in the Wind: The State of Youth Work in a Changing Policy Environment. *Youth & Policy*, 105: 9–36.

Declaration of the 1st European Youth Work Convention (2010) Published on Belgian Presidency of the Council of the European Union. Accessed 30th March 2011 http://www.coe.int/t/dg4/youth/Source/Resources/Documents/2010_Declaration_European_youth_work_convention_en.pdf

Development Education Association (2004) *Global Youth Work: Training and Practice Manual*. London: DEA.

DMU (2013) *The State of Youth Work: Exploring the Future of Youth Work and Young People's Access to Social Rights*. Leicester: DMU/Global Hands/COE.

Freire, P. (1972, revised 1993) *Pedagogy of the Oppressed*. Harmondsworth: Penguin.

Freire, P. (1974) *Education for Critical Consciousness*. New York: Seabury Press.

Freire, P. (1985) *The Politics of Education: Culture, Power and Liberation*. New York: Bergin and Garvey.

Freire, P. (1995) *Pedagogy of Hope: Reliving Pedagogy of the Oppressed*. New York: Continuum.

Jeffs, T. and Smith, M.K. (2002) Individualisation and Youth Work. *Youth and Policy*, 76: 39–65.

Jayakaran, R.I. (1996) *Working with the Urban Poor Using Participatory Learning and Action (PLA)*. Madras: World Vision of India.

Joseph, J., Akpokavi, K.B, Chauhan, V. & Cummins, V. (2002) *Towards Global Democracy: An Exploration of Black Perspectives in Global Youth Work*. London: DEA.

Kolb D.A. (1984) *Experiential Learning Experience as a Source of Learning and Development*. New Jersey: Prentice Hall.

North-South Centre (2010) *Global Education Guidelines, Concepts and Methodologies on Global Education for Educators and Policy Makers*. Lisbon: North South Centre.

Sallah, M. (2008a) Black Young People in the UK: Charting the Tensions of Relativism and Dogmatism in Praxis. In: *The Politics of Diversity in Europe* (Eds.) Titley, G. and Lentin, A. Strasbourg: Council of Europe Publishing.

Sallah, M. (2008b) Global Youth Work: A Matter Beyond the Moral and Green Imperatives? In: Sallah, M. & Cooper, S. (Eds.) *Global Youth Work: Taking it Personally*. Leicester: National Youth Agency.

Sallah, M. (2008c) *The State of Global Youth Work in British HEIs*. Leicester: De Montfort University.

Sallah, M. (2009a) Conceptual and Pedagogical Approaches to the Global Dimension of Youth Work in British Higher Education Institutions. *The International Journal of Development Education and Global Learning*. 1: 3, 39–55.

Sallah, M. (2010) Developing Global Literacy and Competence in Youth Work. In: Davies, B. & nBatsleer, J. (Eds.) *What is Youth Work?* Learning Matters.

Sallah, M. (2013) *Evaluation of the Global Youth Work in Action Project 2010–2013*. London: YCI.

Sankara, T. (1987) *Women's Liberation and the African Freedom Struggle*. Speech delivered on March 8, 1987, commemorating International Women's Day. Pathfinder Press.

Smith, M.K. (1994) *Local Education: Community, Conversation, Praxis*. Buckingham: Open University Press.

Smith, M.K. (1997, 2002) 'Paulo Freire and Informal Education'. *The Encyclopaedia of Informal Education*. www.infed.org/thinkers/et-freir.htm.

Taylor, P. (1993) *The Texts of Paulo Freire*. Buckingham: Open University Press.

Thompson, N. (2003) *Promoting Equality, Challenging Discrimination and Oppression*. Basingstoke: Palgrave Macmillan.

Welsh Assembly Government (2008) *Education for Sustainable Development and Global Citizenship: A Common Understanding for the Youth Work Sector*. Cardiff: Welsh Assembly Government.

Williams, S. and Edleston, J. (Eds) (2010) *Connect, Challenge, Change: A Practical Guide to Global Youth Work*. London: DEA.

Woolley, G. (2011) *The Global Dimension in Youth Work: A Conceptual Model*. Derby: Global Education.

Wylie, (2010) Youth Work in a Cold Climate. *Youth and Policy*, 1–8, 105.

Young, K. (2006) *The Art of Youth Work*. Lyme Regis: Russell House Publishing.

CHAPTER 6

Global Youth Work: Sharing Empiric Evidence of its Efficacy

Introduction

Given that there have been many claims about the effectiveness of Global Youth Work as a pedagogical tool to engage young people, very little empiric evidence exists to support such claims. Given the current status quo where the practice of youth work in general, and Global Youth Work in particular, is under severe threat, it is more urgent now than ever to provide scientific evidence backing claims of Global Youth Work's efficacy; not only for policy makers and funders who demand palpable results, but also for youth work practitioners and young people about the potency of this particular educational approach, based on the twin legs of Development Education and youth work.

In this chapter, I will review a number of research projects I have conducted in this field of study; three cases mainly around the state of Global Youth Work in British Higher Education Institutions (HEIs); a Y Care International (YCI) delivered project exploring the effectiveness of Global Youth Work as a pedagogical tool to engage 180 young people involved in gangs, guns and knife crime; and another project exploring the efficacy of Global Youth Work in engaging over 1,000 young people identified as on the margins. Ultimately this chapter will present empiric evidence backing claims of Global Youth Work's efficacy. It must be stated from the outset that this chapter does not have enough scope to discuss all three research projects exhaustively; consequently, whilst the first two will be mentioned briefly, the bulk of the discussion will centre on the Global Youth Work in Action research project, with a particular focus on the perspectives of young people and the perceived efficacy of Global Youth Work. I would like to acknowledge that empirical evidence in this chapter draws upon the Global Youth Work in Action (GYWiA) project delivered by Y Care International from 2010 to 2013 and funded by the UK Department for International Development. The findings from the report are mainly summarised here and readers are advised to access the full report for more details.

Review of previous studies

There has been some recent research around Global Youth Work, specifically for example Cotton (2009) who mapped out Global Youth Work in the non-formal sector for the DEA. It concluded that 'Youth Work is an excellent vehicle for the delivery of global education and that through Global Youth Work, youth workers can meet a range of mainstream and societal outcomes' (Cotton, 2009: 2). An Ipsos MORI Research Study on behalf of Development Education Association (DEA) (2008) explored young people's experiences of global learning and concluded that over 50 per cent of the sample interviewed have experienced global learning over the previous year whilst 78 per cent felt that schools can help students to understand how they can 'make the world a better place'. Most of the research conducted in this area, however, has been within the field of teacher training (see for example Shiel and Jones, 2004; Scott-Baumann et al., 2003; Martin, 2004; Robbins et al., 2003; Davies et al., 2004). As already reported in Sallah (2009a) two exceptions to these are Lashley (1998) and Joseph (2005). Both of these studies attempted to find out how GYW is covered in English HEIs which deliver youth and community work courses. Lashley (1998) examined 15 institutions, out of which 60 per cent offered GYW sessions, although most of these were one-off sessions, with little opportunity to explore the global dimension in any meaningful depth. The study by Joseph (2005) looked at nine institutions and concluded that GYW is understood differently by different HEIs. This suggests that one HEI might be covering the issue in a way that raises the political consciousness of future youth workers, and at the same time another might be following curricula that reinforce an understanding of relationships to the global South based on charity and dependency. Both reports conclude that youth and community work courses in England could benefit from more quality resources and external support. My research (Sallah, 2009a) went further than these previous studies by involving all four nations of the UK, as well as engaging a wider sample.

Dare to Stretch (2009) has also recently looked at how Development Education is promoted in youth and community work courses in the University of Ulster, Northern Ireland. This research report recommended the incorporation of the global dimension in youth worker training and explored issues of resources and placement.

The state of Global Youth Work in British HEIs research

Over the past five years, I have been involved in conducting research to establish, or otherwise debunk claims of Global Youth Work efficacy. My first piece of research involved finding out the state of Global Youth Work in Higher Education Institutions in the UK.

Conducted between April and November 2008, the research drew partici- pants from Higher Education Institutions across Britain, some of the leading organisations in the Development Education field as well as recent graduates of JNC and equivalent qualifying courses. This research was a collaborative project between De Montfort University, Global Education Derby and DEA. Fifty potential interviewees from institutions offering higher education level youth work courses were identified from across the United Kingdom. From these 50 identified, 43 module/course leaders took part in this research. The second element to the overall approach was a focus group comprised of 11 representatives from a range of organisations:

- Two staff from national charities (1 chief executive, 1 manager)
- Two staff from statutory youth services (2 workers)
- Two staff from universities/training providers (1 principal, 1 lecturer)
- Three staff from international organisations (2 co-ordinators, 1 officer)
- Two final year students

28 recent graduates of JNC or equivalent qualifying courses from 15 HEIs took part in semi-structured telephone interviews. This was a dimensional sample that took into consideration course level and geographical location. Eight graduates had studied up to foundation degree level, 17 had completed an undergraduate programme and three had completed post graduate studies.

A number of important lessons can be drawn from this research. First, it is significant to note that 73 per cent of HEI respondents cited the growing influence of globalisation as a driver for Global Youth Work, which indicates a significant awareness of the need to produce globally literate graduates in a rapidly changing world. This is linked to 54 per cent identifying as an influence the needs of the field which in turn is linked to the need to produce globally literate citizens. Another significant finding is that 46 per cent identified as an influence the individual interest/drive of an individual member of staff; it has been suggested that where a passionate member of staff exists within a team, then the global agenda is given prominence within the curriculum; consequent- ly their departure can also lead to diminishing attention given to the global dimension. It is also significant to note that only 29 per cent of respondents have been influenced by NYA recommendations and LLUK NOS; perhaps this is an area that needs to be worked on.

Resources

Eighteen participants felt that they did have the resources required to adequately train youth workers in the HEIs interviewed, whilst nine felt that they did not have them. Twelve were not sure whether they had adequate resources or not, or felt that they have some resources but not enough, and four did not respond. The responses from HEIs indicate that even those who felt that they did have adequate resources, were willing, open and eager to have more resources available. It was largely acknowledged that some resources already exist and the DEA (now Think Global) website was quoted a number of times, however the vast majority stated that a lot more resources could be made available.

Two main suggestions came from the focus group: first, that HEIs should better utilise the resources of INGOs like Oxfam, Y Care International and the British Red Cross, especially in working with them to place students in these organisations for their field practice. It was also suggested that HEIs could make use of the expertise of INGOs to attract visiting lecturers. It was also stated that whilst there might be some resources generally for GYW, there was not much explicit material for HEIs and this needs to be addressed. Twenty-one percent of HEIs identified the need for good literature and journals whilst 32.5 per cent identified the need for links/guest lecturers from INGOs. Other resources identified as needed include games/simulations, international links/pro-grammes, manuals that give practical resources, centres of excellence to promote GYW and specific resources for HEIs in terms of finance, staffing, time, training and ongoing support.

Skills

In relation to skills, there were two views advanced with equal vigour. Some respondents strongly made the point that teaching Global Youth Work required no extra skill to those already possessed by lecturers and that the same set of skills being utilised in youth and community courses across the UK are more than adequate; one such view is reflected in the quotation below by a respondent:

Nothing specific but generic skills for interaction with students. I couldn't think of anything in terms of skills that would be specific to that particular field of study beyond the generic skills that they need to interact well with students in the classroom.

(Respondent 1, Q16)

On the contrary, other respondents suggested that another set of skills is needed in being able to make the personal, local, national and global (PLiNG) connections:

> *It's about being skilled in being able to make those links between the global, international, national, regional and the local . . . on top of all the other skills you need to be an effective formal and informal educator.*

(Respondent 16, Q16)

The curricula that are included in modules that are perceived to constitute Development Education/Global Youth Work are many and varied, with an identified lack of consistency and correlation between institutions. Furthermore, between institutions, it could be argued that there is a wide disparity between the emphasis and importance that is placed on this topic. Some institutions felt that they made reference to it within other modules; some had half modules with Global Youth Work, whilst others still included a whole module dedicated to this subject. In relation to the impact that this has on professionals that are entering the field of youth work as qualified practitioners, it is important to gauge what organisations (including INGOs, third sector and statutory bodies) feel are essential components for students and therefore practitioners to have an understanding of, prior to their being able to practice Global Youth Work. The findings of this discussion are identified in Table 6.1.

A significant amount of time was spent by the focus group identifying the areas that should be covered in relation to Global Youth Work by academia. The focus group was somewhat representative of the field and therefore identified the current needs of the field. It is essential for HEIs to recognise these identified needs and reflect them in the courses that are delivered, to ensure that qualifying youth workers are adequately equipped to meet the needs of the field and therefore not only to make more employable practitioners but also to enable them to better engage with young people in relation to Global Youth Work and its many facets. The feedback from HEI interviewees suggests that currently the curriculum is far more diverse than this, however, and there is a high level of disparity in terms of what it included, the depth to which it is included and the level of inclusion on qualifying programmes of this topic.

A fundamental issue raised throughout the research is whether Global Youth Work should be a standalone module or integrated throughout the courses. It may be argued that Global Youth Work is good youth work that is inclusive

Table 6.1   Global Youth Work curriculum areas

Item	Curriculum area for consideration by HEIs
Disasters and emergencies Conflict	Conflict and disaster
Diversity Global citizenship Youth citizenship Citizenship	Diversity and identity
Health HIV/AIDs	Health
How can we make links between issues facing young people in this country and overseas Making the personal, local, national and global (PLiNGs) links Global interconnectedness	PLiNG
Critical understanding of the world Construction of social reality Critical reading Critical literacy Intercultural learning	Construction of social reality
Youth justice Global inequalities Bretton Woods Institutions Human rights Rights of the child Anti-discriminatory practice Colonialism	Equality/inequality
Sustainable development	Sustainable development
Process and concept of globalisation Responses to globalisation Historical context	Process and concept of globalisation
Constructive alignment (approach) Social movements (knowledge) Practice skills (skills) Planning global projects (actions)	Method of engagement/practice

and holistic, and as such that it should be an integrated component of *all* modules on qualifying programmes. However, given the depth of material that organisations have suggested needs to be understood and included (see Table 6.1) then it is pertinent to wonder whether this topic needs and warrants a module of its own in order to ensure that students have a good level of awareness and are able to demonstrate understanding of the application of this awareness in their own professional practice.

Fundamentally, this research gives a snapshot of the state of Global Youth Work in British HEIs as of 2008 and raises many cardinal issues around: concept and terminology; skills, knowledge and resources; as well as a proposed curriculum for Global Youth Work. Whilst it points to many strengths in relation to the preparedness of students graduating from JNC qualifying courses to effectively deliver Global Youth Work; it also identifies a number of areas for development around methodology and curriculum areas.

Gangs, guns and knives crime research

The second project was conducted between 2010 and 2012. The project engaged 180 young people aged 11–24, although the overwhelming majority were between 14 and 21, in twelve different sites; seven of them in youth work settings and five of them in Secure Estates. The participants, 25 per cent females and 13 per cent British Minority Ethnic, with an average age of 16.72 were usually engaged in two-hour sessions over a number of weeks. Sixty-seven young people were engaged in the first year and 113 in the second year.

Using a range of evaluation tools including project worker evaluations, young people's individual evaluation (response rate of 66 per cent), observation visits and semi-structured interviews, I was able to capture relevant data to gauge the effectiveness of the project intervention. This project was ground-breaking in its ability to engage young people at the margins to deconstruct their realities and make local-global connections to their lives. Some of the key findings from the evaluation include:

- Seventy-two per cent of respondents claimed an increased awareness of gangs and violence outside of the UK, towards the end of the project, which represents a 36 per cent change during the project.
- Fifty-two percent increase in young people feeling that they were better able to illustrate local-global links towards the end of the project.
- The number of young people feeling that they were able to stop gang, gun and knife violence increased from 9 per cent to 29 per cent.

- Overall, 97 young people responded to the question about the impact of the project on them. 77 per cent reported that the project had made them less likely to join a gang, 51.5 per cent reported that the project had made them less likely to carry a knife, 48 per cent reported being less likely to carry a gun and 51.5 per cent reported being less likely to commit a crime. Only about 4 per cent of respondents reported that the project had not made any impact on them.

This research is significant in a number of ways; not only in its ability to engage young people perceived to be 'hard to reach' and 'disengaged', but also in using the pedagogical tool of Global Youth Work as an educational approach that has demonstrated efficacy in provoking consciousness and resulting in commensurate action by young people. The evidence from the above research illustrates, from young people's perspectives, the potency of Global Youth Work in engaging them.

Global Youth Work in Action

The Global Youth Work in Action (GYWiA) project was designed by Y Care International to provide spaces outside of the formal education system for marginalised young people, to increase their understanding, empathy and interconnection with global issues, international development and poverty; as well as support them to take action as a result of a change in behaviour, commensurate with their abilities.

The GYWiA project directly engaged a total of 1,197 young people mostly between the ages of 16 and 25. During the lifespan of the project, there were thirty-three delivery partners from a range of settings and dealing with a multitude of marginalised young people including those with less than five GCSEs, socio-economically deprived young people, and young people marginalised because of their sexuality, disability, nationality and or other social stratifications. Global Youth Work as a methodological approach was used to engage given groups of young people, over different time spans, to explore local-global issues through an informal, creative and participative approach to learning.

Project overview

Y Care International is the international relief and development partner of the YMCA movement in the UK and Ireland. Since 1984, it has worked in partnership with young people across the world to respond to the needs of the most marginalised in society. As part of its Global Youth Work programme, YCI works with marginalised young people in the UK and Ireland to help them explore global issues that are relevant to their lives. Following a successful project award from the Department for International Development to YCI, the Global Youth Work in Action project started on the 1st April 2010 and ended on the 31st March 2013. The project also planned to increase the capacity and confidence of youth workers to plan, deliver and evaluate Global Youth Work with young people; however we will not be covering this dimension of the research here due to lack of space.

The project was a response to several needs, including the need of marginalised young people to access global learning, the need to support Global Youth Work outside the formal education sector, and the need to link up the youth work sector which has traditionally been disjointed in its approach to Global Youth Work.

Project objectives

The project objectives were as follows:

1. 1,050 marginalised young people will have increased awareness, knowledge and understanding of development issues and how they relate to their lives and the lives of young people in the global south.
2. 1,050 marginalised young people will have increased skills and confidence to be active global citizens and share their understanding of global issues amongst their peers, communities and wider society.
3. 122 youth workers will have gained capacity and skills to develop, deliver and evaluate youth-led projects that explore development issues.
4. 42 youth work organisations will have increased motivation, skills and capacity to run projects that build support for development.
5. A further 2,100 members of the wider communities in which the projects take place will have an increased awareness of development issues and the role individuals can play to reduce poverty overseas.
6. The wider youth work sector has access to independent academic research, including evidence from the project, on the impact of Global Youth Work on young people and the wider society.

Evaluation methodology

A range of evaluation methodologies were used to capture the effectiveness or otherwise of the project in relation to the project objectives. The researcher and the YCI project managers were keen to make sure that evaluation was an inbuilt mechanism from the start of the project and not something added on as an afterthought at the end of the project. From the initial conception of the project, through to the funding application and project implementation, the researcher worked with the YCI project management team to design, refine and amend the evaluation methodology as appropriate. The evaluation methodologies went through a piloting stage, and feedback from respondents was used to improve the initial methodologies.

YCI established through its reports from youth workers that 1,197 young people were directly engaged through the grants programme for the duration of the project. However, in terms of collecting individual and aggregate data from the project participants, there was a response rate of 55 per cent, falling to 39 per cent for individual-level data. Furthermore, not all the young people completed each and every question in the evaluation form at either individual or aggregate level. This was due to a myriad of reasons, including: the difficulty in tracking down the young people once the projects were nearing the end; the transient nature of the lives of many of the young people; their own choice not to participate in the evaluation; the skills of the youth workers in explaining the evaluation to the young people and/or facilitating the participatory data collection sessions; and the culture of collecting evaluation data from young people within the project partners. Caution therefore must be exercised in relation to the degree to which this information can be generalised to all participants. However, it is imperative to note that invaluable data was collected from young people, capturing their demography, project learning and reflections as well as skills and knowledge gained.

In total, 44 project workers from 33 different projects across the three years completed Youth Worker Reflection Forms at the end of their projects via the online monitoring and evaluation system. All 33 projects submitted reports at the end of their projects, sometimes preceded by interim reports. This was a set template distributed by YCI with spaces for project managers to report on the project overview, profile of participants, financial expenditure, workshop activities and outcomes, and workers' reflections on Global Youth Work activities and outcomes. A total of six semi-structured interviews were conducted by the researcher, two projects from each of the years.

Demographics

Over the three years, based on the individual and aggregate data of the project, the young people were mainly of white heritage, making up 54 per cent of respondents; and there were 364 women, making up 55 per cent of respondents. Where individual and aggregate data is available, more than two thirds of participants were aged 15–25. Within this, the largest age range (36.8 per cent) was 15–18 years-olds at the time of the project, followed by 28.9 per cent being aged 19–22 at the time of the project.

Measures of social exclusion

The project specifically aimed to engage young people who were traditionally seen as 'marginalised' or hard to reach. YCI focussed on attempting to engage young people from areas of high levels of deprivation, who had experienced some form of discrimination (e.g. disabled young people, those from ethnic minorities or from LGBT groups) or who were confronted by some other forms of challenge which could lead to social exclusion (e.g. being an asylum seeker or refugee; having insecure housing and/or living in social housing; young people with substance misuse experience). YCI recognise that this would be best described by the projects which worked with the young people directly. Over the project's lifespan, the majority of young people engaged were from marginalised backgrounds.

Thematic analysis

In presenting the analysis of the findings, five dominant themes were identified, as follows, and we will go on to discuss them to demonstrate the efficacy of Global Youth Work (I have chosen not to report on the fifth theme, as this is focused on the workers rather than on the young people):

1. Young people's understanding of development issues and lives of young people in the global South.
2. Impact of GYW on young people and wider society.
3. Added value of Global Youth Work to developing active global citizenship (skills, confidence and knowledge).
4. Young people taking action within their communities and the wider society.
5. Youth workers and youth work organisations developing capacity, motivation and skills.

1. Young people's understanding of development issues and lives of young people in the global South

The first objective of this project was to support 1,050 marginalised young people to increase their awareness, knowledge and understanding of development issues and the interconnectedness of their lives to those in the global

South. Evidence gathered from the evaluation report suggests that a minimum number of 1,197 young people were engaged over the lifespan of the project. The evidence gathered also further suggests that the awareness, knowledge and understanding of the young people in the project, as evidenced in the individual young people's evaluation forms, the project workers' reports and the semi-structured interviews, has been profound in a number of ways.

Furthermore, the data from individual young people's interviews strongly shows that 98 per cent of young people believed that their knowledge of global development issues increased over the lifetime of the project. The majority of young people (62 per cent) felt that this increase was by 'some' or 'a lot'. This suggests the project met its key goal, at least among the young people who completed the evaluation forms. In the qualitative dimension of the young people's individual evaluation forms, there is ample evidence to illustrate the links the young people made as a result of undertaking the project. The following quotes from young people over the three years demonstrate the profound impact of the project on them:

The most important thing learnt during the project

It was all important and relevant information. I was not aware about child soldiers before the project and it made me think about these young people in different parts of the world.

(Participant, Yr 1, Cardiff YMCA)

It put things into perspective of things that happen in this country and the importance of helping others that don't get any support.

(Participant, Yr 1, City of Belfast YMCA)

The most important thing I learned during the project was the shocking statistics and information on AIDs and HIV. Also the techniques to educate peers on the awareness of this global issue.

(Participant, Yr 1, Derby Interfaith Forum)

The most interesting thing that I learnt about global development during my project was the different causes and effects of war and what we could do to help.

(Participant, 2nd Yr. Cyfanfyd)

That by buying fair-trade, even if you choose to only replace one product you normally buy with a fair-trade one, you are consciously supporting farmers and other hard working individuals. It highlights how our choices when buying food and other commodities can help others too.

(Participant, Yr 2, Made in Europe)

About understanding the truth behind sweatshops, and how people are being paid for jobs unfairly e.g. making footballs.

(Participant, Yr 3, SREC)

Rules of other countries on homosexuality.

(Participant, Bournemouth YMCA, Yr 3)

It was surprising to hear about the gang culture in the UK, I was surprised as I thought gangs were mainly in America, it made me think about what a Gang is!

(Participant Midlands YMCA, Yr 3)

Increase in awareness, knowledge and understanding (reported by youth workers)

Throughout the whole project we were talking about how the things we do here affect everybody. We looked at case studies about different areas around the globe and how the young people in those areas are affected by the things that people do all over the world, and how climate change affects everybody everywhere, so they were aware that it's not just here in Britain.

(Project Worker, Sutton Coldfield YMCA)

We saw the end video together and the striking conclusion was that there wasn't a great deal of difference (laughs) because the two young women who were depicted in the video, whilst they might have had different lives materially, the struggles and the challenges were much the same. So, lack of access to education for the Zimbabwean girl – for whatever structural reason – the girl who was depicted in the UK had to re-sit A levels to get into university so she too was struggling. Although she had access to public benefits, it wasn't easy for her.

(Project worker, Inspirational Journeys)

Young people's reported change in behaviour potentially impacting on the global South)

The project also appeared to have met its goals regarding engendering a change in the global behaviour of young people. From the individual interviews we can see that 65 per cent reported that they had made 'a lot' or 'some' change in their global behaviour in years 1 and 2. The figure falls to 60 per cent in year 3. However, across the three years, 91 per cent stated that their global behaviour had changed, the majority (63 per cent) of these by either 'a lot' or 'some'. The types of global behaviour change amongst young people varied and were anecdotal but many reported buying Fair Trade products or signing up to charity campaigns as examples of how their behaviour changed. Global Youth Work, as a pedagogical tool, appears to have affected young people's behaviour.

2. Impact of Global Youth Work on young people and wider society

It is imperative to reflect on how GYW has impacted on young people from project workers' perspectives.

> *It was an idea . . . to draw on their own experiences of sport because many of them were actually born in other countries. So the project was also very much about looking at ethnic diversity and sport and drawing on the participants' experiences of what sports they'd actually played in their countries of origin, any cultural or identity-based issues to do with particular sports and also looking at sport in the UK, particularly football and we were looking at football and racism as well and looking at sport again, particularly football, although it's experienced lots of racism over the years it's also a very powerful tool to bring people together, and for community cohesion.*
>
> (Project worker, Somerset Racial Equality Council)

> *We went to the CAT centre in Wales; it's a centre for alternative technology. We stayed there for 2 nights in a little cabin where we had to produce our own electricity to heat it and light it and provide our hot water and everything. It was sort of this little cabin, it was built into the mountain. It was ever so nice. And on that project while we were at the CAT centre, it's got a lot of information about alternative technology and how we can slow down climate change. So we went round all the stuff that you can do there and we also had a session with one of their lecturers on wind turbines and we made our own little wind turbine and learned how to make the most effective ones.*
>
> (Project Worker, Sutton Coldfield)

3. Added value of Global Youth Work to developing active global citizenship (skills, confidence and knowledge)

During the project, we also explored the young people's learning about development issues in schools prior to the project intervention. Across all three years, most of the young people (72 per cent) had either learnt 'not at all' about development issues at school or learnt a 'little'. 75 percent and 80 per cent of respondents fell into this category in year 2 and year 3 respectively; a notable exception to the trend was year 1 where 56 per cent reported that they had learnt 'a lot' or 'some'. The significant majority of young people who responded to this question stated they learnt either nothing or 'a little' about development issues in school, furthermore only 7 per cent reported learning 'a lot'. Young people were asked about the most important thing they had learnt from the project, and they reported as key learning: learning about different countries and other young people; understanding of global inequality; seeing things differently as a result of reflection; and understanding global interdependence. The following quotes illustrate young people's learning and the impact of the project on them.

Learning about different countries and other young people

Learning about Rwanda and the Hutus and the Tutsis.

Most important thing I have learned is probably about other countries and what the difference between them and my country is.

I learned a lot more about the different global issues that are in the world from different people's thoughts on different issues.

The different cultures that exist in the world.

I have learned more about the issues that affect Togo, as I was not aware of it before. It was really interesting to how diverse it is.

Hearing about what happens in countries we can't visit.

Inequality in the global South

That the pesticides that are used to damage illegal crops can kill animals and children.

That people make our clothes for like 60p.

Bad work conditions and terrible pay in other countries.

I learned how it is difficult for people in poor countries to protect themselves but that it is even more important for them because HIV is more common in the developing countries.

Companies make large profits cos they use child labour.

Reflection – seeing things differently

There's not only poverty in a country. Even a country that has the reputation of a poor country has rich parts.

The amount of people who go hungry every day compared to how much food people waste really blew me away.

I didn't realise that I could play a part in the world, I now know that little things that I do can achieve something.

That it's not only girls get trafficked, its old people and men too.

The most interesting thing that I learnt about global development during my project was the different causes and effects of war and what we could do to help.

I also learnt that there is other positive things that people can do to help other countries, instead of just sending food parcels!

Understanding of global interdependence

We also learnt about how different foods and drinks are produced around the world and who makes the money from them.

It was all important and relevant information. I was not aware about child soldiers before the project and it made me think about these young people in different parts of the world.

I learned how much each country is actually connected and actually affect each other.

How many people drug trafficking actually affects.

Skills and confidence

Learnt how to protect myself against HIV and other STIs.

The most valuable skills learned were teamwork/leadership skills and management skills, that have given me the confidence to continue and think about other similar projects.

Emotional responses

That we are not doing enough to support those who are less fortunate, small changes in our lifestyles can make dramatic positive changes to theirs.

The conditions the children work in, was sad to see.

Active global citizenship (developing skills, confidence and knowledge – from workers)

I think one of the main things for me was to see how far they'd come and how much they'd learned unconsciously as well. They'd just learned so much over the course of the project; it really prepared them to carry on and do things, like applying for jobs. Because before they didn't have those skills; now they have.

(Project Worker, West Bromwich YMCA)

Well I think that was the conversations they were having in school and in their classrooms and then going home. And even the fact that they were aware that there was something called Fair-trade, for me, is a small step, when they were coming in from communities that would have no link, or no apparent links to anything in the global south and wouldn't have any real understanding or comprehension of the context in global youth work terms, to actually know something about it and to go home and have the confidence to say, 'Mum I was doing this today in school and I'm just wondering, do you know where that banana comes from? Do you know where that coffee that we're buying comes from? And do you know where my clothes are coming from?' So the fact that they were even aware and did have the confidence to say that to their parents. And then for them to come in to us and say, 'I heard this news report on the news. Was that what we were talking about last week?' So the fact that their awareness was being raised in that sense. And when we asked, a few of the kids – but not all of them, because some had enough to deal with their home life – coming in and telling us that these conversations were being had. It was a very small step in terms of their journey in confidence and skills in relation to global issues, but it was momentous for us coming in, when they had no knowledge and no awareness whatsoever.

(Project worker, Belfast)

It empowers young people because they become more aware of global issues but, because it's a global issue, even though it is taking place within their own country, because it's taking place 'over there' they feel that there's very little that, as an individual, they can do about it, because, generally, the young marginalised people we work with tend to feel disempowered anyway which is obviously why we do what we do in terms of trying to develop confidence and things like that. And certainly some of the conversations I've had with young people, it promotes a political conversation. So a conversation I had with a young person was around, 'What are governments doing about it? How do we lobby government? How do we do this and do that?' And it makes them realise that there are elements to this society that are quite profoundly sick. And there are things that should be being done by the powers that be that aren't. And so it motivates them and empowers them so they are armed with knowledge, but it also disempowers them because the hierarchy already know about it but not enough is being done about it, so they can become quite ticked off about it.

(Project worker, Derbyshire YMCA)

The quotes above illustrate only a small percentage of the increased awareness and learning from the perspective of project workers and it is important to juxtapose this with the increase in knowledge reported by young people. There is overwhelming evidence to suggest that young people's awareness, knowledge and understanding has dramatically increased as a result of the project intervention.

Teamwork, communication and listening were the most common responses to skills learnt throughout the project lifetime. The fact that these are a much higher percentage than skills such as writing and maths could suggest that learning occurred 'by doing' (discussions and working together) rather than through more formal, didactic learning methods.

Project participants significantly rated their confidence highly in the use of skills gained over the project. 83 per cent, 89 per cent and 80 per cent respectively in year 1, year 2 and year 3 reported 'a lot' or 'some' confidence to use these skills gained over the project, which averages at 84.2% of participants over the three years.

Further analysis of the individual level data gives more details on these trends. Females appear to be more confident in the use of skills gained through their participation in the project. As can be noted from the data analysis, 43 per cent of the population who were females had either 'a lot' or 'some' confidence in the use of skills gained. This significantly exceeds the male side where only 37 per cent of the total population affirmed they had either 'a lot' or 'some' confidence using skills gained on the project.

There was about average activity in the participation of young people in Global Youth Work activities, according to the individual and aggregate data, like awareness raising and campaigns. Thirty-two percent had taken part in an activity in year 1 rising to 64 per cent and then falling to 55 per cent respectively in years 2 and 3. This would appear underwhelming considering that respondents appeared to have been highly confident of their abilities to use their new skills as reported earlier. However this can be explained by the fact that some action might have been taken later on without the project being able to report on it. However, it can be said that there has been able ample evidence to demonstrate that a significant number of young people have started making the transition, as the second prerogative of my theory of provoking consciousness and supporting action advocates, to leaving that state of hopelessness and powerless, to change the way things are. The following quotes illustrate the shift in conceptualisation.

I have learnt the potential we all have to make a difference even if it is just a drop in the ocean. I have also become aware of global issues I did not know existed and have seen first-hand those working hard to make the changes.

(Participant, Derbyshire YMCA)

I never knew that I could do anything to stop poverty. But even little stuff like signing an action card can help.

(Participant, Restless Development) Source: Tier Two (individual and aggregate data)

4. Young people taking action within their communities and wider society

We did that workshop, filmed the workshop and made it into a resource pack and the resource pack will be available and designed for youth workers across the UK, and will be free to every YMCA in the United Kingdom.

(Project worker, Derby YMCA)

A lot of our young people live independently or strive to live independently and I think that's something – even where they live with their parents they now do recycling – because I've noticed they will bring their recycling in from home to use our bins.

(Project worker, Sutton Coldfield)

We had feedback from the teachers who would say, one of the schools had given them each a country to go and research in the global South . . . one of the teachers came back and said, even the language had changed, it wasn't 'poor black babies' which is always the language we have been accustomed to here. I mean, I remember collecting money for 'the black babies'. That's what it was called, 'The black baby collection'! So even their language changed, and she said there just seemed to be a greater understanding of some of the issues that we had brought up.

(Project worker, Belfast)

We also had a video at the end which presented our findings of the views of the locals and why immigrants move over here, so we'd asked some questions to everybody that they came into contact with. The majority of people had been fine, we were lucky to find a set of people who didn't mind being filmed and we filled out a consent form for that. And then at the end when we got the video editor to come in, we had all these clips. He sat down with them and showed them how to edit the video and they looked at the clips of people to see which ones they thought had more impact than others or had more relevance than others and then they put the video together as well.

(Project worker, West Bromwich YMCA)

In relation to taking local-global action after the project, there is no data entered for the first year, however in the second and third years, significant changes were reported by respondents especially in the area of fair-trade/ ethical consumerism: 'We wrote a letter to Tesco's to tell them only to buy fair trade chocolate and now that's all I buy, and I give my clothes to charity instead of throwing them out' (Participant, Portadown YMCA, 3rd Yr).

There was also significant action reported in the young people's evaluation in: signing petitions, donating or volunteering for fundraising or charities, turning off lights and plugs at home, recycling and creating awareness through conversation.

Why Global Youth Work is effective

It is cardinal at this juncture to reflect on the use of Global Youth Work as a methodology and why it has been highly effective in engaging young people, especially some of the most marginalised on this project. The project participants over the three years often spoke of informal learning through games and play, learning by doing like making a DVD, organising a fundraising for Syria, making T-Shirts, being on a residential, making a CD, going to the Houses of Parliament, going to a Masjid, going on the radio, to making clothes. These varied spaces of learning as reported by the participants provoked their appetite to learn beyond the traditional context of schooling. This situation of learning in informal and non-traditional spaces makes learning 'fun' and engaging.

Another project participant captures this: 'I enjoyed going to the different youth clubs across Cardiff to do our workshops. I also enjoyed the boat party on the London trip (Rolling Globe) where we met other young people' (Yr 1, Bournemouth YMCA).

New learning or 'learning new things' is possibly the most mentioned constant in answer to the question posed to all the participants who responded to the young people's individual evaluation, 'What was the best thing about the project?' The responses suggest that there was a generation of curiosity and that Global Youth Work as a pedagogical tool has been largely successful in engaging the disengaged, which has been able to engender critical learning/literacy and generate 'new experiences' of being able to 'view the world in someone else's eyes' (Participant, Yr 3, SREC). The learning, as reported by respondents, was also of a kind that often stretched their knowledge: 'learning about the different types of gangs from the Mungiki in Kenya to the numbers gangs in America' (Participant, Midlands YMCA) made the participants eager to engage.

Another important dimension of Global Youth Work is the positioning of young people as co-producers of knowledge – 'teaching and making others aware of what's going on' (Participant, Yr 1, Bournemouth YMCA). A critical analysis of the qualitative dimension of young people's responses suggested that this pedagogical approach to engagement did not consider education as something to be done to young people but something to be done with them.

This educational approach of positioning young people as co-producers of knowledge means they take ownership of the learning process and are invested in the venture, rather than reproducers of knowledge and subjected to what Freire (1972) calls 'banking education'. Across most of the projects evaluated, there was a conscious effort to 'tip the balance of power' (Davies, 2005) in young people's favour and equalise the power imbalance.

Moreover, young people often felt able to take action after the intervention. A young person captures this view:

> . . . *doing something. I've always felt frustrated and sometimes powerless in not being able to do something about the issues in the world. It feels good, even though it's on a small scale, to be able to be part of the process in solving some of those issues.*

> (Participant, Made in Europe, 2nd Year)

This can be constructed as a symbiosis between consciousness and action, 'being able to speak out'. This linkage of existence and consciousness; learning and action; provoking consciousness and taking action, is the hallmark of good Global Youth Work.

A significant number of the young people also reported that meeting people from different places and backgrounds was a key ingredient for learning; especially in the spaces and opportunities provided by the different dimensions of the project.

Conclusion

In concluding this chapter, it is pivotal that we reflect on a number of key issues. We have reviewed three major research projects in the field involving: the state of Global Youth Work in British HEIs; a research project exploring the deployment of Global Youth Work as a pedagogical tool to engage young people involved in gangs, guns and knife crimes; as well as another research project exploring the efficacy of Global Youth Work in action to engage young people on the margins. All of these research projects are against the background of a dearth of research in this field and therefore provide much needed empiric evidence to demonstrate the potency of Global Youth Work. Whilst two of the three projects focused on young people on the margins, the pedagogical approach of Global Youth Work must be understood as a tool for all young people. It can be argued that we have provided empiric evidence to illustrate the efficacy of Global Youth Work. Additionally, as argued in the theoretical section, the research bears that Global Youth Work is distinct because it is rooted in informal learning by doing; provides varied learning spaces; focuses on generating curiosity and stretching the minds of young people; positions young people as producers of knowledge; supports young people take action; and addresses local-global issues.

References

Cotton, N. (2009) *Global Youth Work in the UK: Research Report.* London: DEA.

Dare to Stretch (2009*) Promoting Development Education in Youth Work Training, A Research Report on Development Education in Community Youth Work Courses at the University of Ulster, Jordanstown.* Belfast: Centre for Global Education.

Davies, B. (2005) Youth Work: A Manifesto For Our Times. *Youth and Policy*, 88: 1–23.

Davies, L., Harber, C. and Yamashita, H. (2004*) Global Citizenship Education: The Needs of Teachers and Learners. Research Report.* Birmingham*:* Centre for International Education and Research, School of Education, University of Birmingham.

Freire, P. (1972) *Pedagogy of the Oppressed.* Harmondsworth: Penguin.

Ipsos MORI Research Study (2008) *Young People's Experiences of Global Learning.* London: DEA.

Joseph, J. (2005) *Collated Summary of Questionnaire Responses.* Unpublished Report for the National Youth Agency/Critical Praxis.

Lashley, H. (1998) *Report on the Study of an Understanding of Global Youth Work.* Unpublished Report for the Training Agencies Group.

Martin, F. (2004) *Providing a Global Dimension to Citizenship Education: A Collaborative Approach to Student Learning Within Primary Initial Teacher Education.* Research Report. Accessed 16th February 2010 at: http://www.citized.info/pdf/commarticles/Fran_Martin.pdf.

Robbins, M., Francis, L.J. and Elliott, E. (2003) Attitudes Toward Education For Global Citizenship Among Trainee Teachers. *Research in Education Journal*, 69: 93–8.

Sallah, M. (2009a) Conceptual and Pedagogical Approaches to the Global Dimension of Youth Work in British Higher Education Institutions. *The International Journal of Development Education and Global Learning.* 1: 3, 39–55.

Scott-Baumann, A., Holden, C., Clough, N. and Hicks, D. (2003) The Global Dimension in Education. *The Development Education Journal*, 10: 1, 15–18.

Shiel, C. and Jones, D. (2004) Global Perspectives in Higher Education: Taking The Agenda Forward in a Business School. *The Development Education Journal*, 10: 3, 10–12.

Conclusion

Reflections

In this concluding section of the book, I intend to share my reflections on the overall narrative of the book as well as my encounters in research, practice, teaching and policy making; and how these encounters have come to shape my thinking and practice. I wish to share my innermost thoughts on the urgent matters this book seeks to address. Global Youth Work as a discipline belongs to that set of disciplines that focuses intervention on the objective of provoking critical consciousness and generating critical literacy as a first priority; individual and collective realities are the site of this struggle and contestation. This can imbue a sense of vulnerability and unpredictability in demanding an extreme transparency in relation to one's values and philosophical underpinnings; and them being subjected to critical interrogation by others. In this light, Global Youth Work can generate uncomfortable spaces; additionally it can never be conceived of as a complete project like learning how to ride a bike; it must always be seen as an incomplete and fluid work in progress.

To set the transparency ball rolling, my motivation for writing this book has been to locate this emerging discipline within: a plethora of ways of working with young people, Development Education, the dilemmas of globalisation, as well as working with the dispossessed (of the basic necessities of life and hope). It has been rooted in my practice and the many realities I breathed, both living in the South and North and having my conscience pricked again and again, both in my professional and personally realities. From living under Bretton Woods conditionalities in The Gambia in the 1980s to staying in the French suburbs in the 2000s, I have borne witness to horrible and unimaginable human suffering that need not be. These situations, and many more scenarios of structural violence, too graphic to narrate, have led to me resolving to do something about the way things are; these conditions are neither acceptable nor inevitable, we can do something to change them. This innate desire for social justice is what influences my writing, thinking and practice. Global Youth Work, for me, must first and foremost be about challenging social injustice; it should be a vehicle to build a better world. It can never be an instrument of indoctrination; it should be about generating critical dialogue and must also never be ashamed to be upfront about its foundation of social justice.

In **Chapter 1**, we established that globalisation is contested, fluid and differently interpreted; as Scholte (2005) argued, the only agreement around globalisation is that there is no agreement of what it means. We also established that both the concept and process of globalisation are now givens in theory and practice, but as to whether it is a force for good or bad, the jury is still out. We argued that whilst globalisation has been used in many instances as a force for good, it still remains largely premised on Northern hegemonic dominations over the South, propelled by the Washington Consensus, serving as a basis for launching structural violence on the vast majority of the world's peoples indiscriminately. Some would argue that globalisation has made great strides, for example the number of people in China living on less than $2 a day fell from 634 million to 212 million between 1981 and 2001 (UN, 2005) but this masks the true nature of within country inequality as well as ignoring the dire situation in other parts of the world like Sub-Sahara Africa.

In **Chapter 2**, we illustrated that an understanding of globalisation is preconditioned on constructed reality, often on the basis of negative neutrality. In a globalised world, where dominant configurations of ways of knowing and being are constructed from Eurocentric and dominant perspectives economically, politically, technologically, culturally and ecologically, then development and its attendant consequences are also constructed and enacted according to a vision through these lenses. Hence the significance of the construction of social reality cannot be underestimated, as what then comes to be seen as right and wrong, good and bad, just and unjust are conceptualised and enacted within these local, national and global spaces, giving hegemony an everlasting source of energy. Global Youth Work as a discipline should attach great significance to this deduction, that unless you change the way people see the world, then you cannot change how they interact with it. Global Youth Work as a first step must encourage people to deconstruct and reconstruct their realities through democratic and dialogical processes.

In **Chapter 3**, we painted the picture of a sick world shrouded in social injustice and global equality, where there is a construction of poverty and suffering as normal: from the unequal distribution of the world's resources, where 20 per cent of the world's population consume 80 per cent of the world resources; where global structures like the Bretton Woods Institutions are more interested in maintaining a dysfunctional and exploitative global economic order based on the maxim of 'profit at all cost', rather than genuinely supporting countries to emerge from under-development and disfigured development. We illustrated that the economic, educational, social, political and ecological dimensions of inequality and the attendant consequences of this grotesque abomination are pervasive; we also shared some of the mechanisms facilitating this, like the Bretton Woods Institutions and trade barriers.

In Chapter 4, we advanced the idea of development as an antidote to the status quo, aiming to create a more just and equal world where the earth's inhabitants can access the basics of life and have the opportunity to engage in the pursuit of happiness. A critical look at the models of development revealed a greater focus on the economic dimension and the postulation of the neoclassical model as the dominating world order, premised on the Washington Consensus. Critics of this model, especially from the South, have advanced counter-orthodoxy models, which often largely place an emphasis on the state attempting to control the market, yet subsumed within the prevailing dominant global economic order; development thus becomes a highly contested concept, not only in charting a course for acceptable development but one that is sustainable as well. UNDP (2010) and Sen's (1993, 1999) approach to human development with a focus on capabilities and freedoms shows greater promise with a conceptualisation of development as multidimensional and the different aspects of political, economic, social and health inextricably linked to one another. Development must take a holistic approach and start from the grassroots. It must also be multi-layered in simultaneously launching an assault at the personal, local, national and global levels.

In Chapter 5, we explored how Global Youth Work is situated within a multitude of interventions trying to address the development conundrum. A range of interventions seek to arrest the development dilemma, including those of governments, anarchists, Development Agencies, terrorists and anti-capitalist movements. I would argue that all of these have a similar objective, namely of challenging development orthodoxy and bringing something better; however, what this is and their methods and levels of willingness to employ violence, are different. Global Youth work, as a distinct practice in this light, employs a combination of youth work methodologies and principles and Development Education philosophical approaches. As a distinct approach, it focuses on supporting young people in deconstructing and reconstructing reality, to gain critical consciousness. The second objective is then to support young people, either as individuals or as a collective, to take action that promotes social justice, commensurate with their abilities. Global Youth Work then, is a pedagogical and practical tool that supports young people to explore the impact of the five faces of globalisation on their lives at the personal, local, national and global levels in order to align their existence and their constructed reality (a process of gaining a new and critical consciousness) and then taking action at the personal, local, national and global levels to change the way things are.

In **Chapter 6**, we reviewed a number of research projects exploring the efficacy of Global Youth Work. The discipline and practice of Global Youth Work goes by many names and I have been involved in it in some way over the last 20 years: as a Gambia Red Cross volunteer promising to 'link the world in a chain of human sympathy'; to delivering Global Youth Work sessions and training across Europe; to organising international study visits in the South; to researching and teaching the subject at De Montfort University. However, providing empiric evidence of Global Youth Work's efficacy has always been elusive in the field. I have conducted and presented three ground-breaking research projects over the past five years establishing the efficacy of Global Youth Work. Global Youth Work works in terms of provoking young people's consciousness in seeing the world differently; and often leads to action when they interact with the world differently as a result of this newfound consciousness, following Global Youth Work's intervention. However, it must be acknowledged that these studies were only done in England, Wales, Scotland and Ireland, and therefore have limited generalisability, even though my practice experience elsewhere backs up these findings. Additionally the action young people choose to take can also appear minuscule given the grand and urgent scale of social injustice, whether they are advantaged or disadvantaged by the prevailing world order.

I am aware that some readers might want to throw at me charges of being polemical and of bias in my attempt at opening up, and throwing down a gauntlet for, democratic dialogue. But this is a charge I am willing to embrace, because global social injustice is a matter of life and death for some; it is not just an academic exercise conducted in an isolated Ivory Tower. Practicing Global Youth Work, for me, is breathing back hope into a state of hopelessness and paralysis, provoking consciousness and supporting action; it cannot be an exercise in futility and cosmetic decorations.

References

Scholte, J. A. (2005) *Globalisation: A Critical Introduction*. Basingstoke: Palgrave

Sen, A. (1993) Capability and Well-being. In Martha Nussbaum, C. and Sen, A. (Eds.) *The Quality of Life*. Oxford: Clarendon Press.

Sen, A. (1999) *Development as Freedom*. Oxford: Oxford University Press.

UN Department of Economic and Social Affairs (2005) *The Inequality Predicament*. Report on the World Social Situation. New York: United Nations.

UNDP (2010) *Human Development Report 2010: The Real Wealth of Nations:* Pathways to Human Development. New York: UNDP.

Working with Black young people

Edited by Momodou Sallah & Carlton Howson

978-1-905541-14-0

'Addresses relevant topics with academic rigour and passion. A publication such as th   as been long over due; we would have to go some way back in social work research to find on   f similar depth and quality . . . rich in information and research, and tackles many issues (e.g. rac   dentity, practice, role of voluntary sector organisations, forced marriages, education, community   hesion, etc.) with clarity and commitment to addressing racism in its various guises . . . a pleasure   read... presents debates from historical and contemporary perspectives in a forceful manner with g   : heart . . . a key text.' *British Journal of Social Work.*

This book seeks to challenge both the accepted status quo of Black young people's   jative over-representation in most aspects of British life – including education, criminal justice, hous   j and health – and their underrepresentation in empiric literature. It seeks to help find ways forwa

Contributions from a wide range of practitioners, academics and students all draw on pe   onal experiences and explore a wide range of important issues. Offering opportunities to gain a c   eper insight into issues that confront Black young people – and consider strategies for change   the chapters in this book are sometimes about specific sections of the community but often, and collectively, about the lives of many different people with shared experiences of oppression, immigration history and discrimination.

Working with street children
An approach explored
By Andrew Williams

978-1-905541-80-5

'A book that bridges the gap between academia and know-how.' *Andy Sexton, Associate International Director, Oasis Global, Co-chair 180 Degree Alliance.*

Provides an insight into the work involved – and level of commitment demanded – from anyone working with street children in developing countries anywhere. Based on his work as a very locally involved CEO of Retrak in Africa, British social worker Andy Williams provides an analysis of how one approach was tried, tested, improved and expanded through careful and constant attention to reflective analysis and review; and shows how principles can be drawn out which transcend both culture and the practical application of those principles in any one context. The approach is holistic, relational, transitional, child-centred and professional.

'An introductory text book to a brilliant approach drawing on lots of wisdom and experience.' *Youthwork.*

Radical youth work
Developing critical perspectives and professional judgement
By Brian Belton

978-1-905541-57-7

'Refreshing, honest, provocative, unapologetic, irritating, often challenging and highly recommended
. . . a catalyst for reflection, debate and experimentation in the youth work field at a time when this
is sorely needed.' *Addiction Today.*

How can youth workers support young people while delivering policy?
What makes a 'positive activity' positive?
When is an 'informed choice' truly informed?
Why is politics in education discouraged?
How can we make sense of all of this?

Belton encourages workers to help young people – through questioning – to forsake ready-made
ideas and products and reawaken their own – and our – imaginations, sense of wonder, and faith
in dynamic possibilities.

'What a breath of fresh air to read this book. Not an easy or comfortable read as it pushes the brain
to do some work, but definitely worth the effort.' *Youthwork.*

Includes Tania de St Croix's consideration of a foundation literature of radical youth work, and how
new theories could be engendered.

The art of youth work
Second edition
By Kerry Young

978-1-903855-46-1

'Young's description of the way in which good youth work can instil the key features of critical thinking that underpin educational attainment and the sense of citizenship is about as good as it gets . . . an eloquent, poetic and philosophical reassertion of the unique contribution of the youth work purpose.' *Rapport.*

Power and empowerment
By Neil Thompson

978-1-903855-99-7

Empowerment has become a well-used term across a wide variety of work settings that involve dealing with people and their problems. But is it a central part of good practice or an empty word? And what of power? It is a central theme of human services practice but, like empowerment, is often only loosely examined.

'A useful gateway to the complexity of power and empowerment . . . as succinct an introduction as one could wish for . . . It is a book which speaks a strong commitment to social justice and which also provides a welcome antidote to the tendency to polarise 'powerful' and 'powerless' – Neil Thompson provides an altogether more subtle and compelling analysis . . . I can see experienced practitioners and practice teachers enjoying it. This is a book that goes well beyond the rhetoric.' *Professor Mark Doel, Sheffield Hallam University.*